How to Draw Dragons Step by Step - Volume 1 - (Step by step instructions on how to draw dragons)

This book has over 300 detailed illustrations that demonstrate how to draw dragons step by step

J.P. Manning

1. Drawing a basic grid outline will help you to give your picture good proportions.

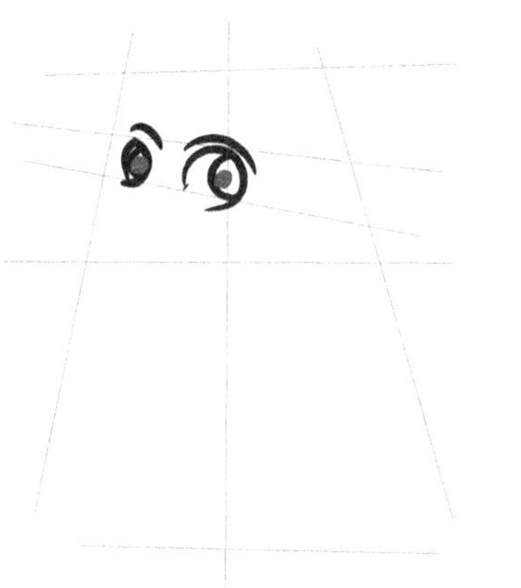

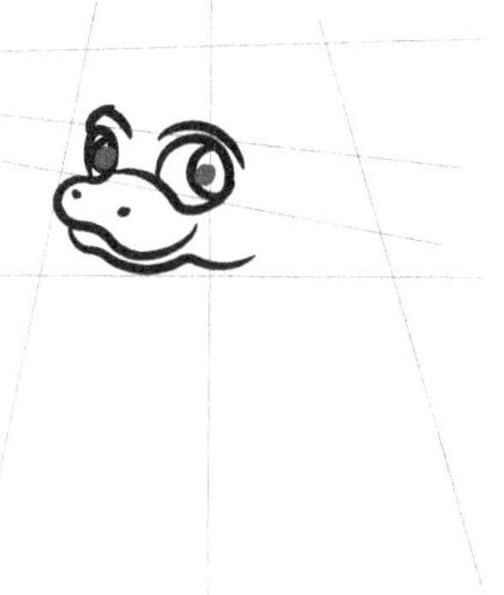

2. Drawing lines on your grid will help you to draw eyes that are focused on a distant object.

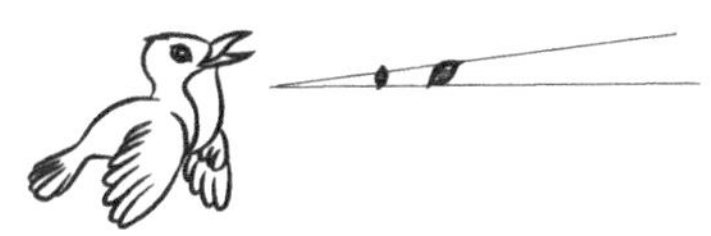

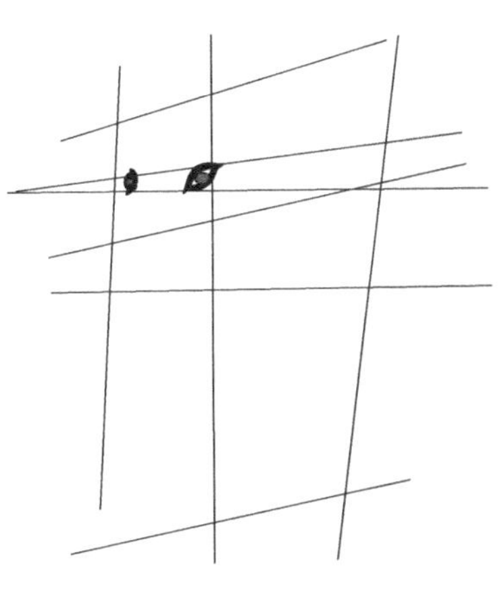

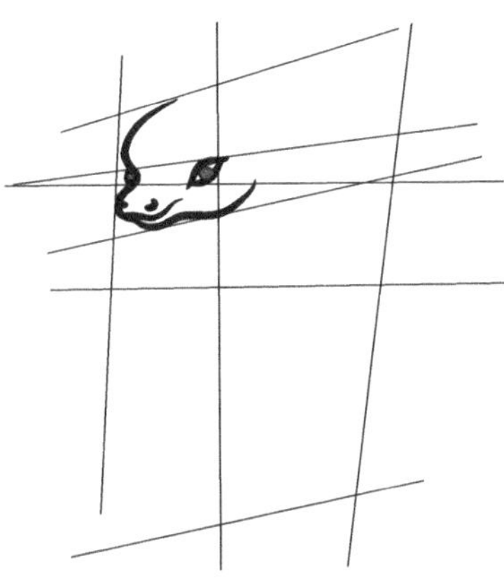

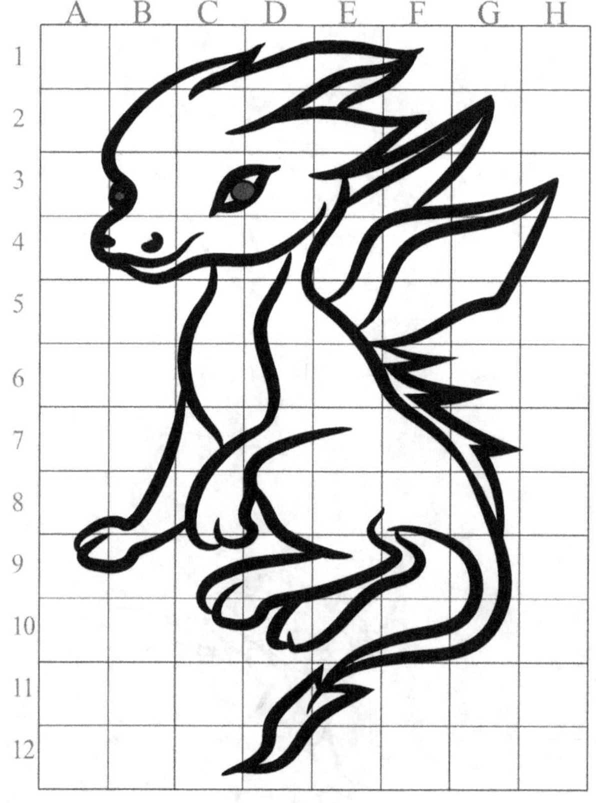

A B C D E F G H
1
2
3
4
5
6
7
8
9
10
11
12

3. Starting your drawing with the eyes will help your initial sketch to take shape.

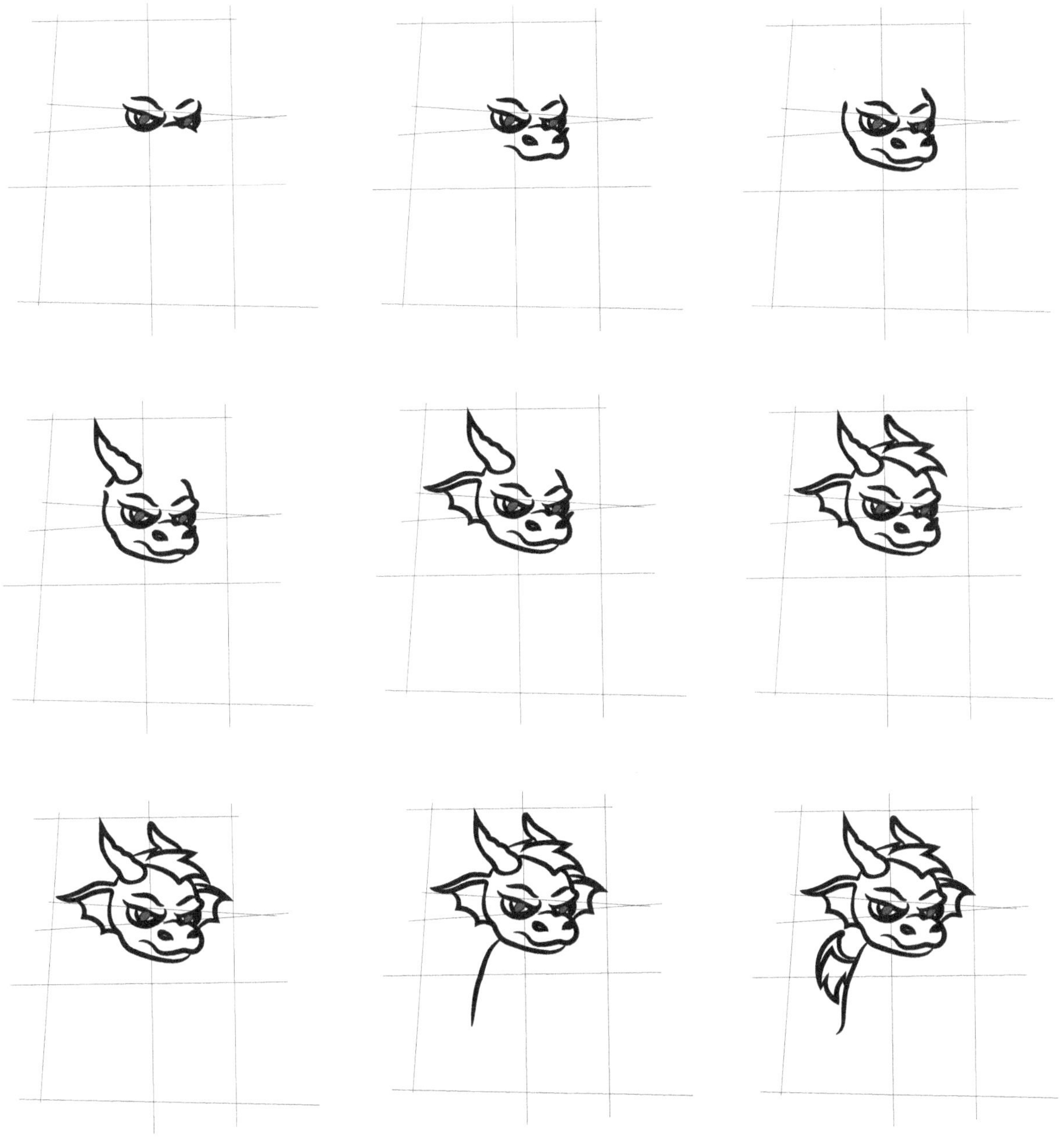

A B C D E F G H
1
2
3
4
5
6
7
8
9
10
11
12

4. Draw the head first and then build the rest
of the body around it.

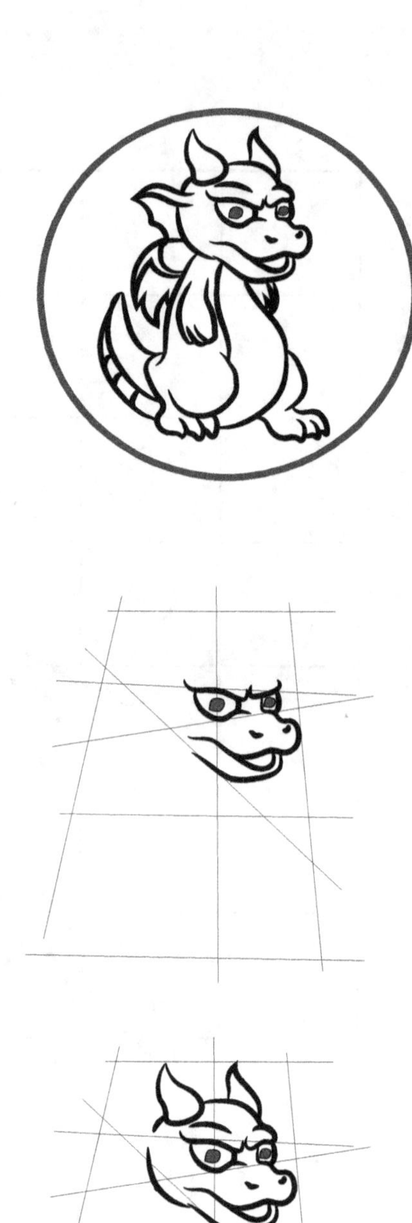

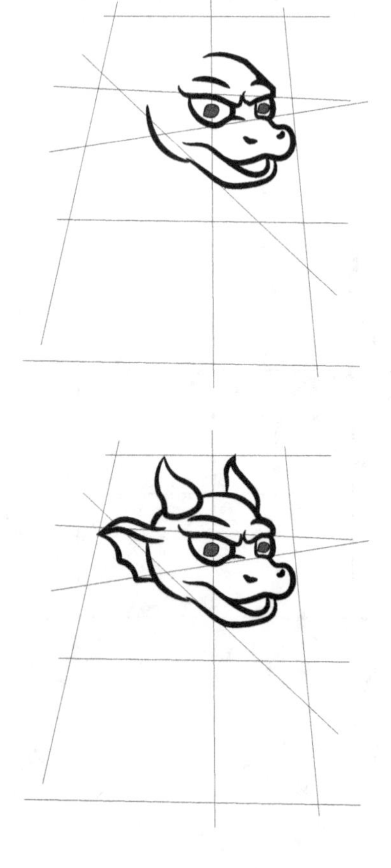

A B C D E F G H
1
2
3
4
5
6
7
8
9
10
11
12

5. Separate your grid into sections to help you decide how you want to proportion your drawing.

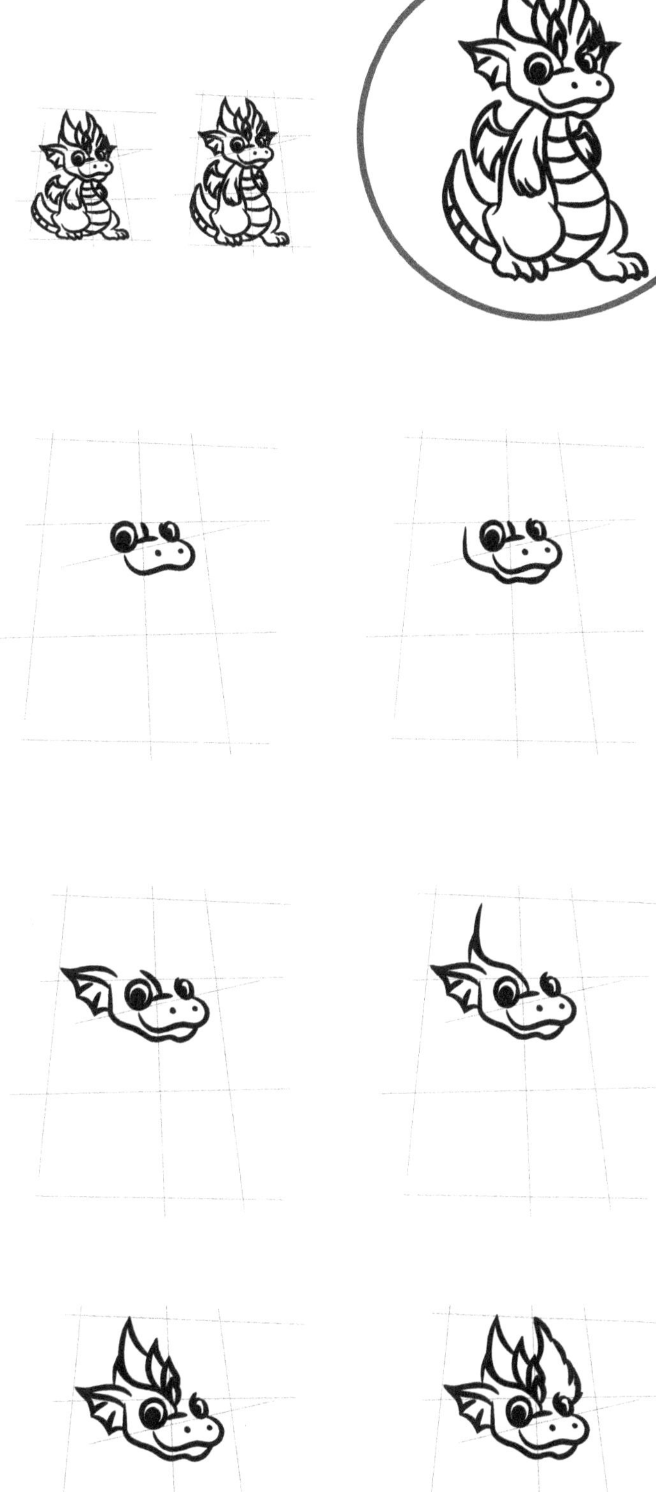

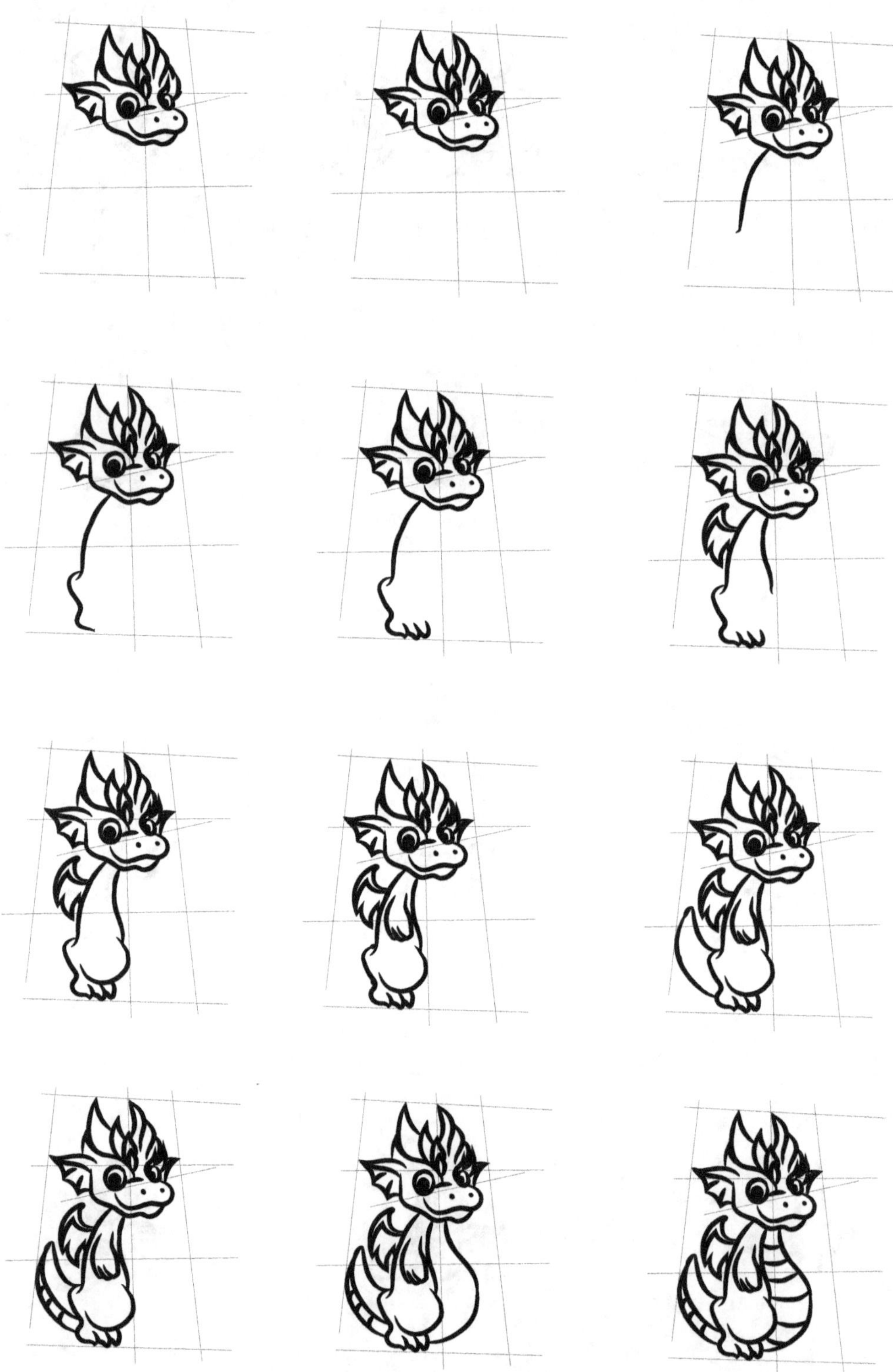

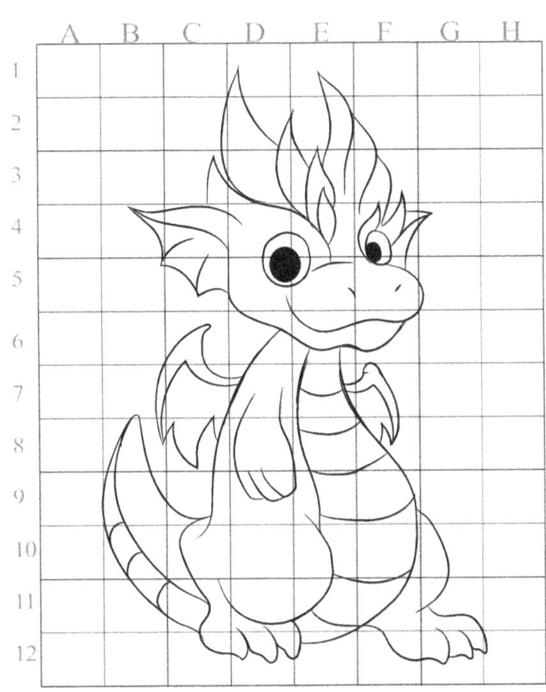

6. Flame coming out of your dragon's mouth can produce a very nice effect.

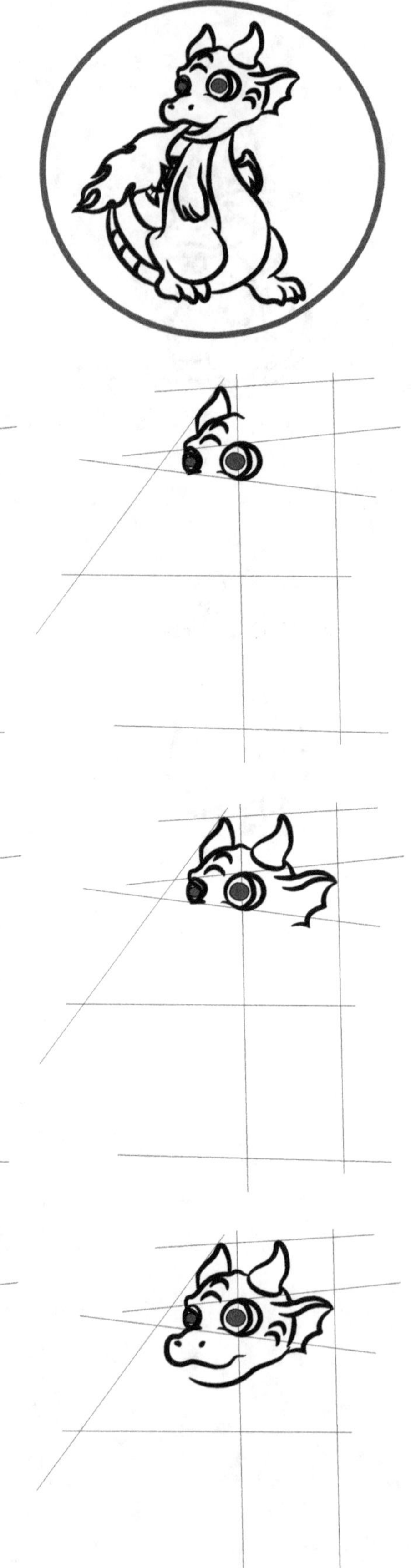

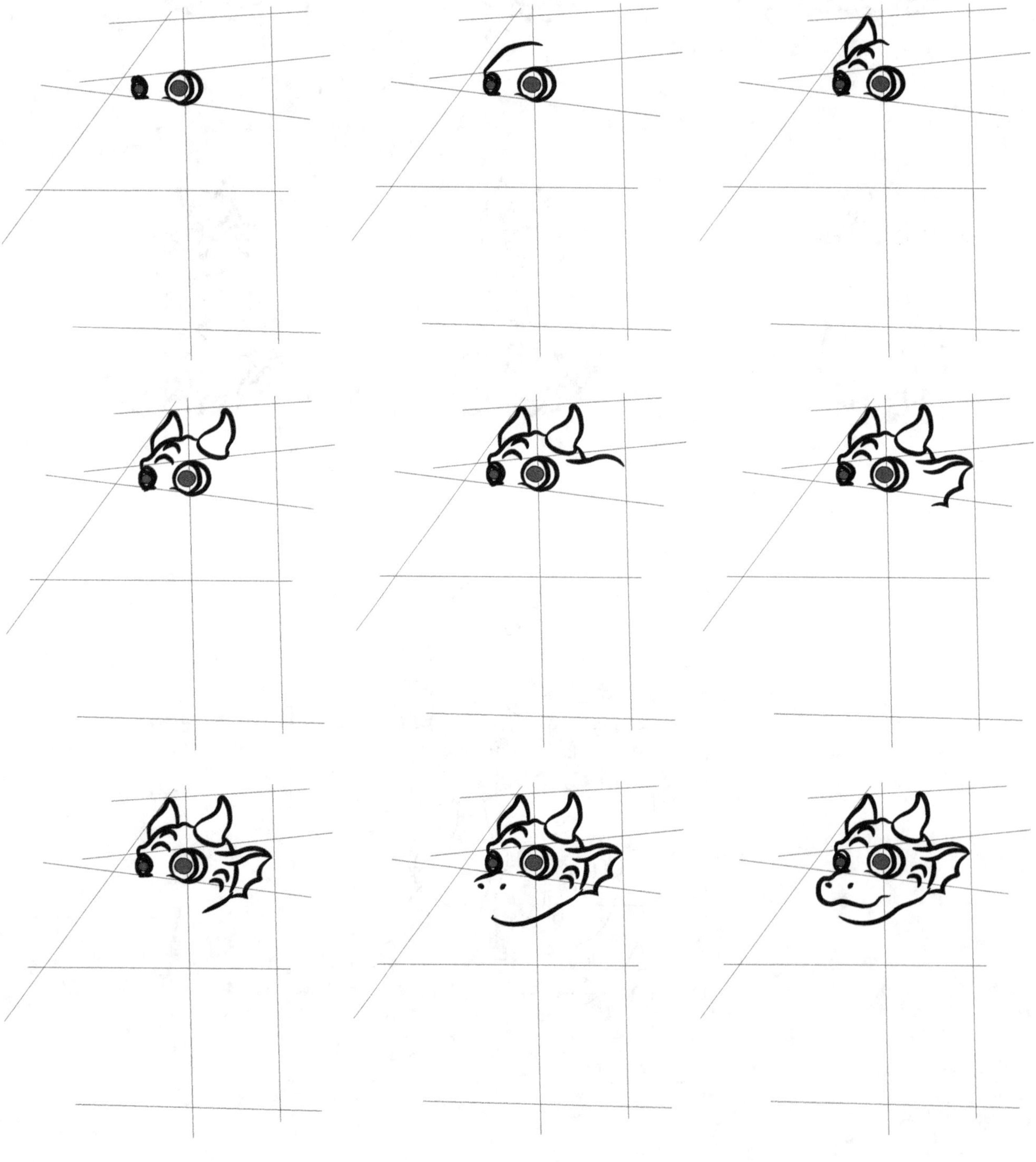

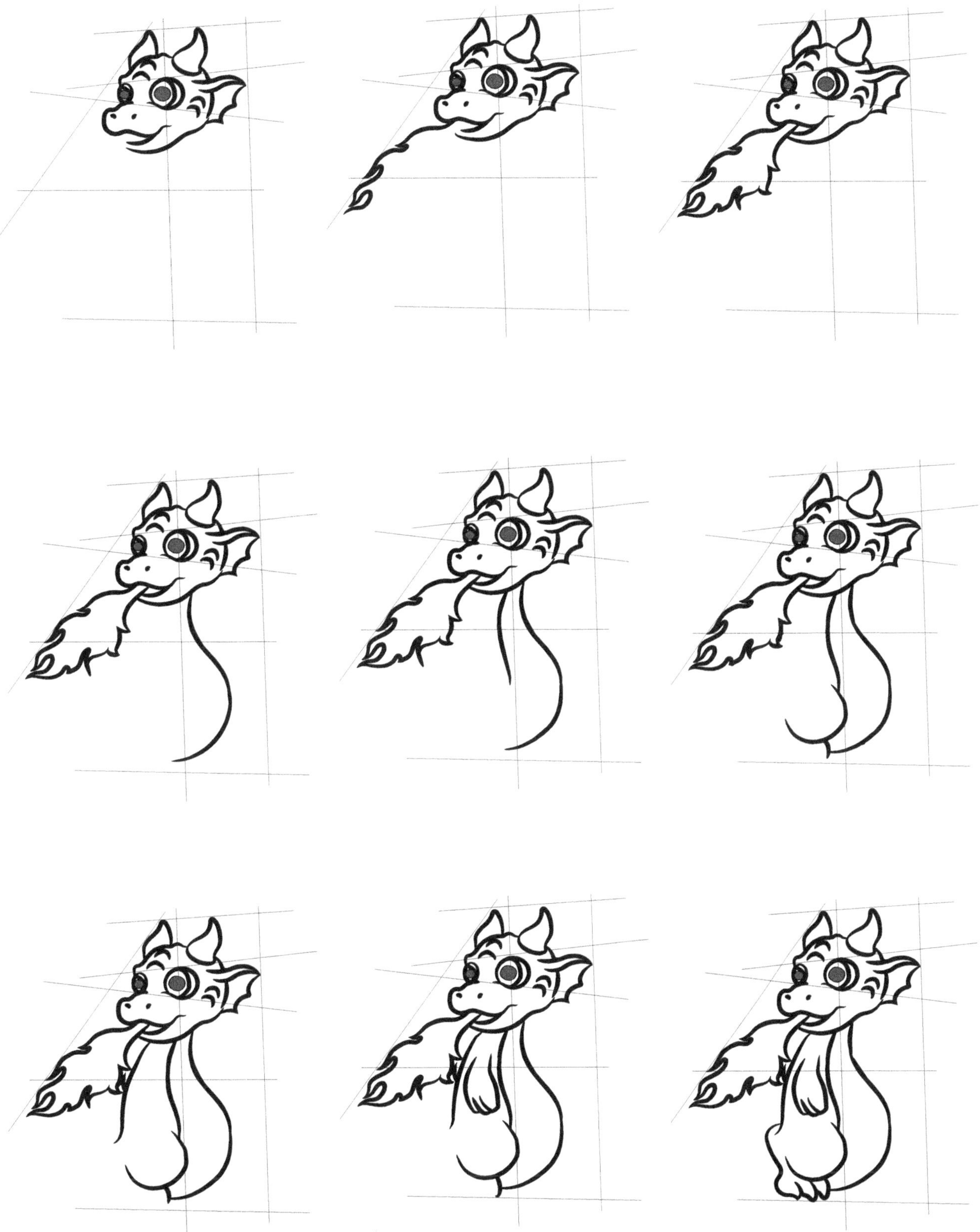

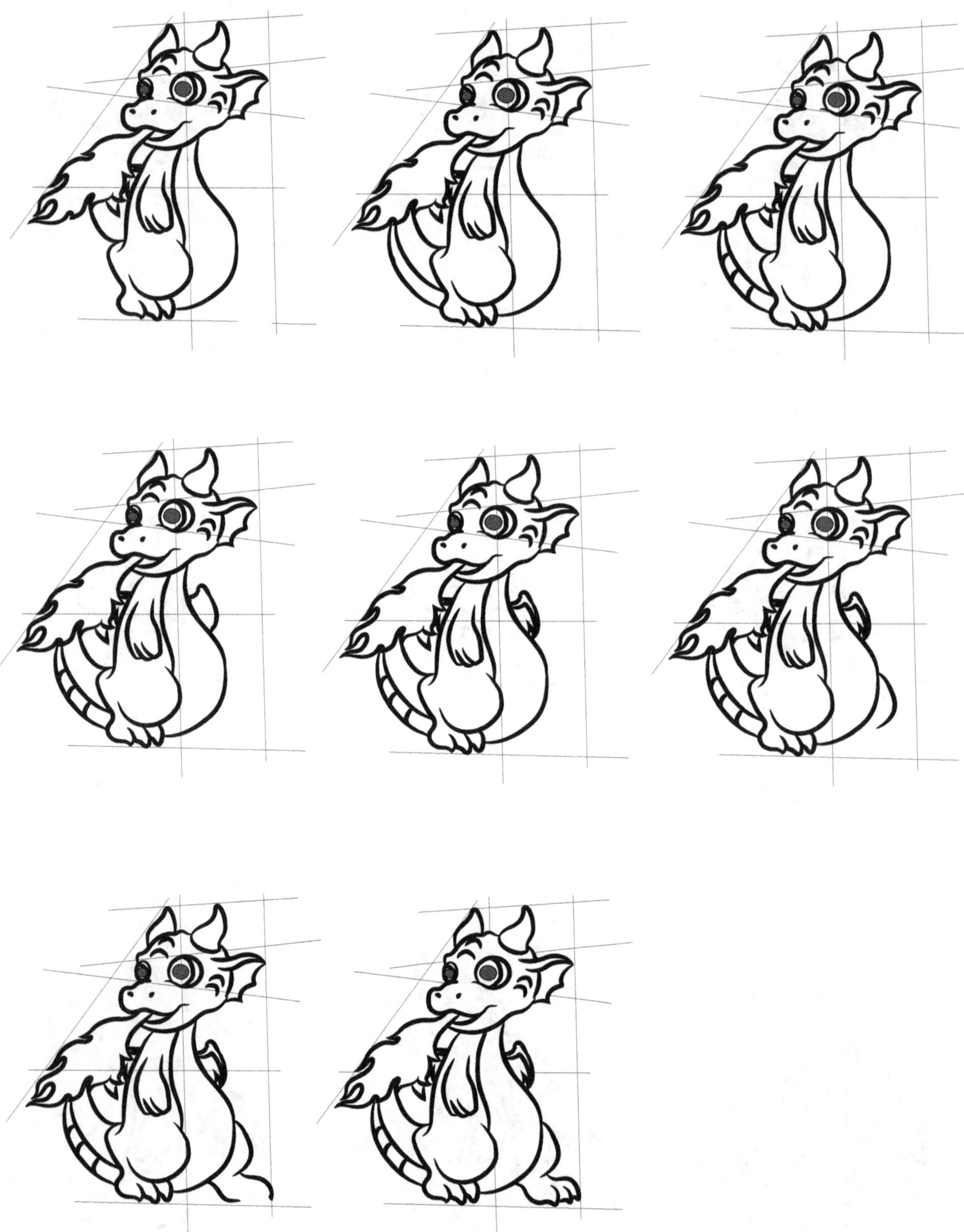

A B C D E F G H
1
2
3
4
5
6
7
8
9
10
11
12

7. Drawing a curved line
on your grid can help
you to keep your
dragons tale on track.

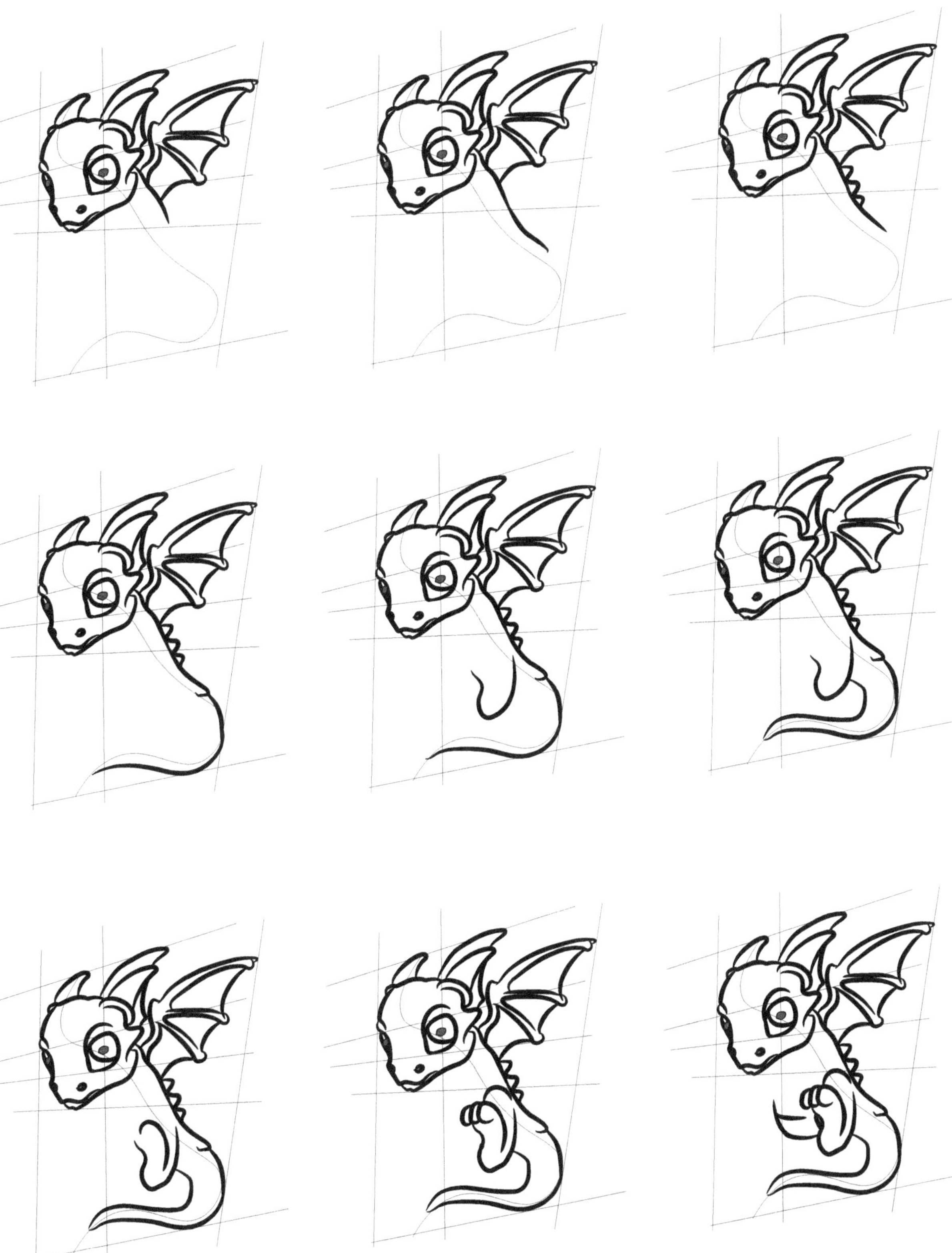

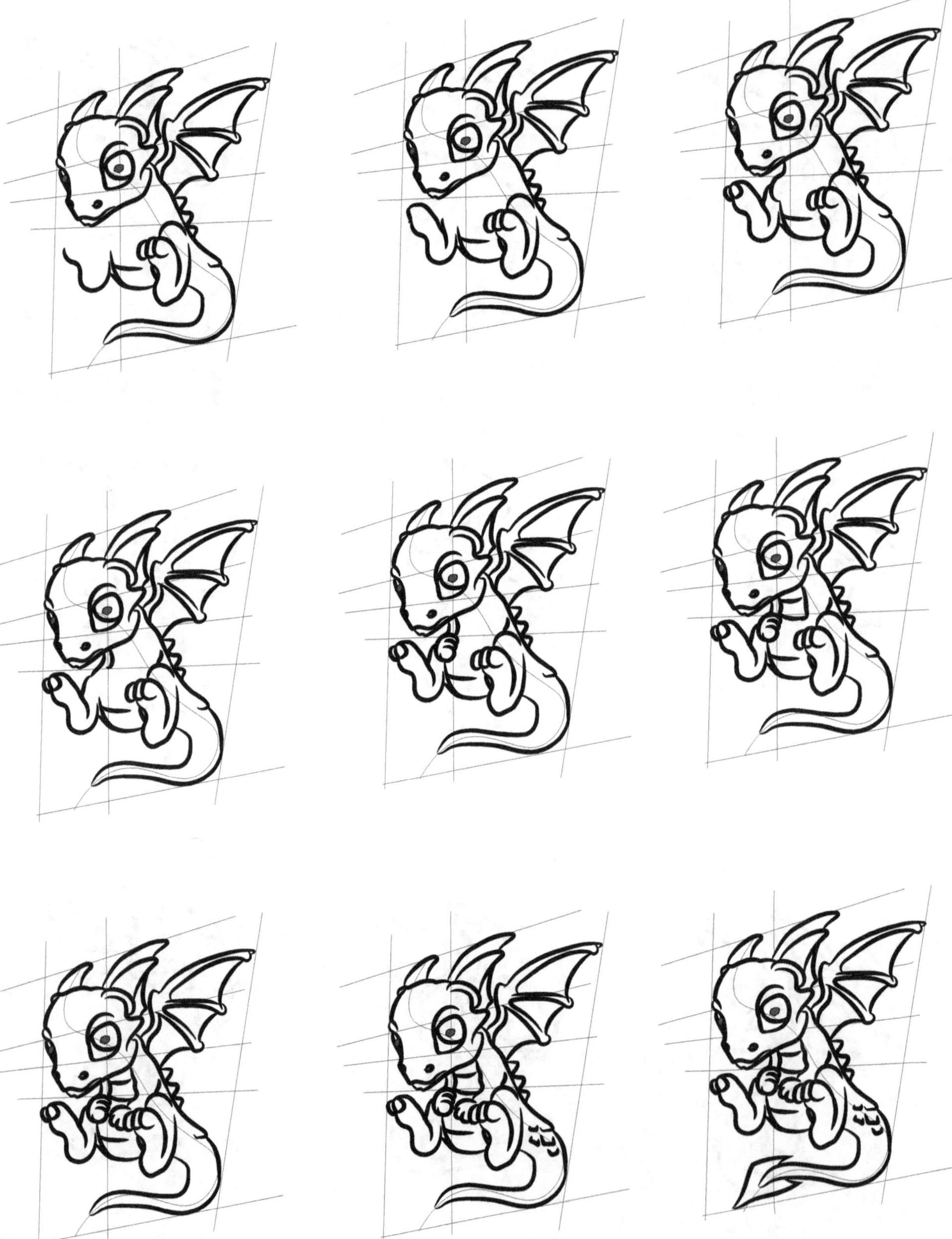

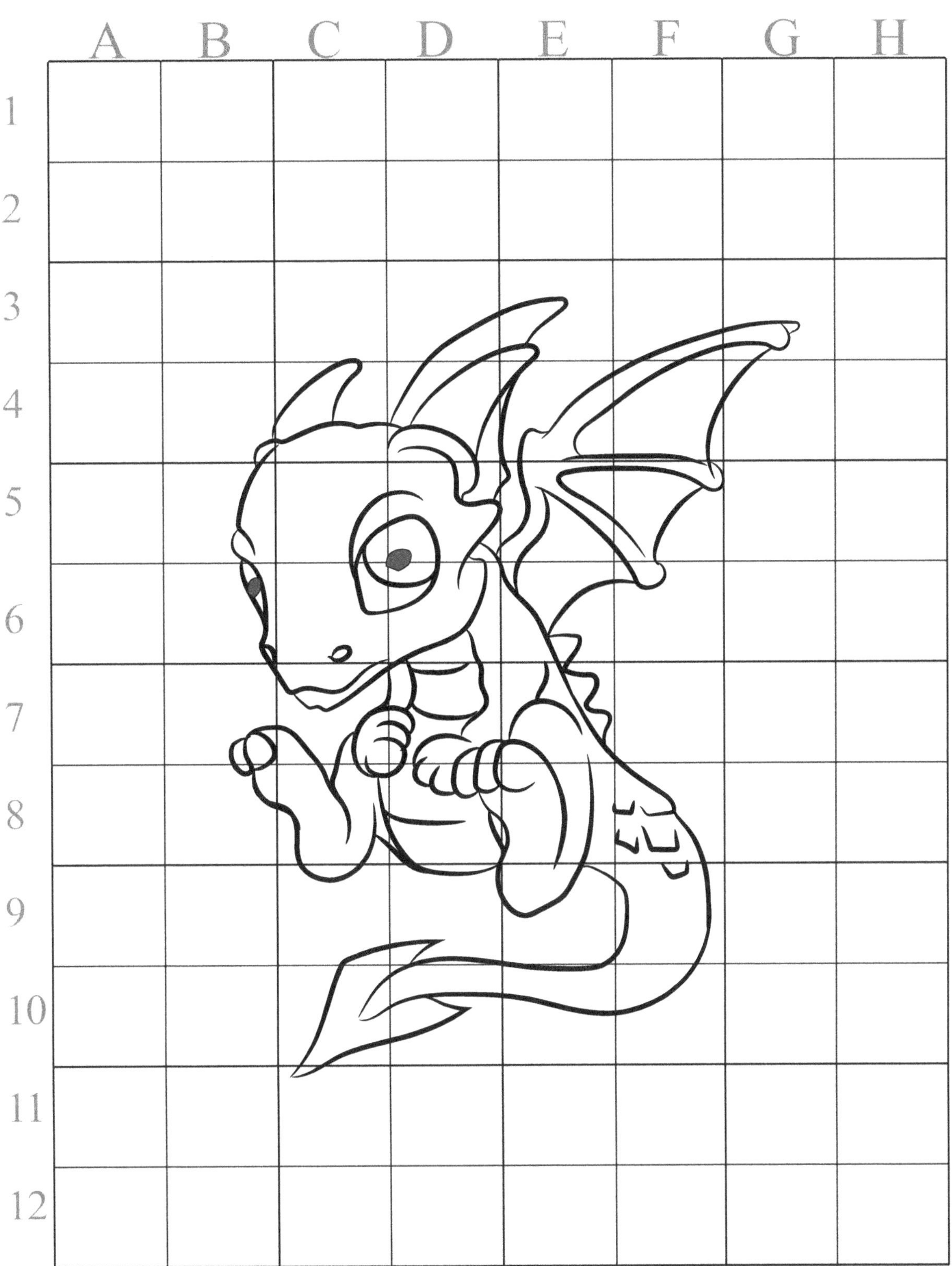

A B C D E F G H
1
2
3
4
5
6
7
8
9
10
11
12

8. Drawing a basic grid
outline will help you to
give your picture good
proportions.

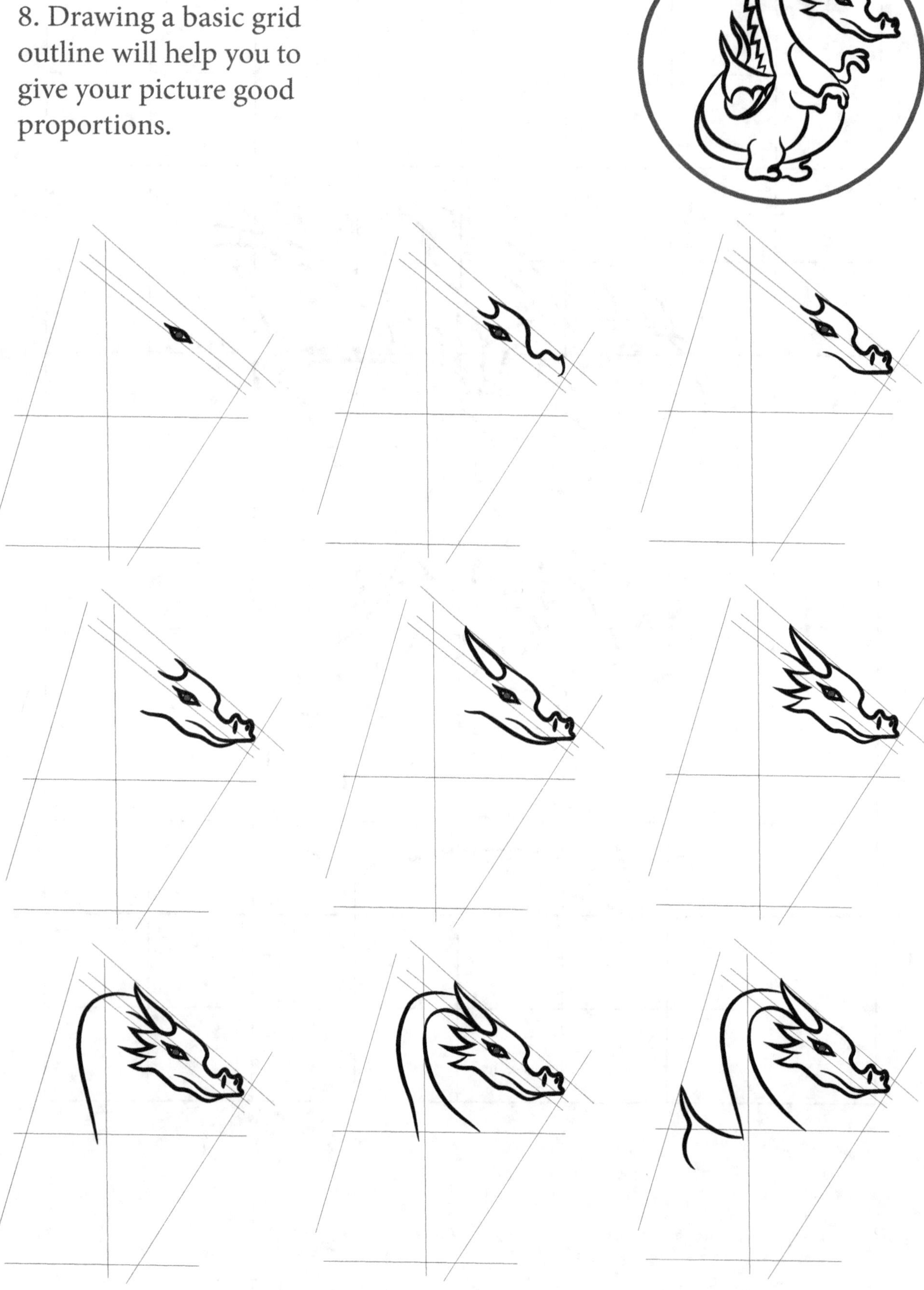

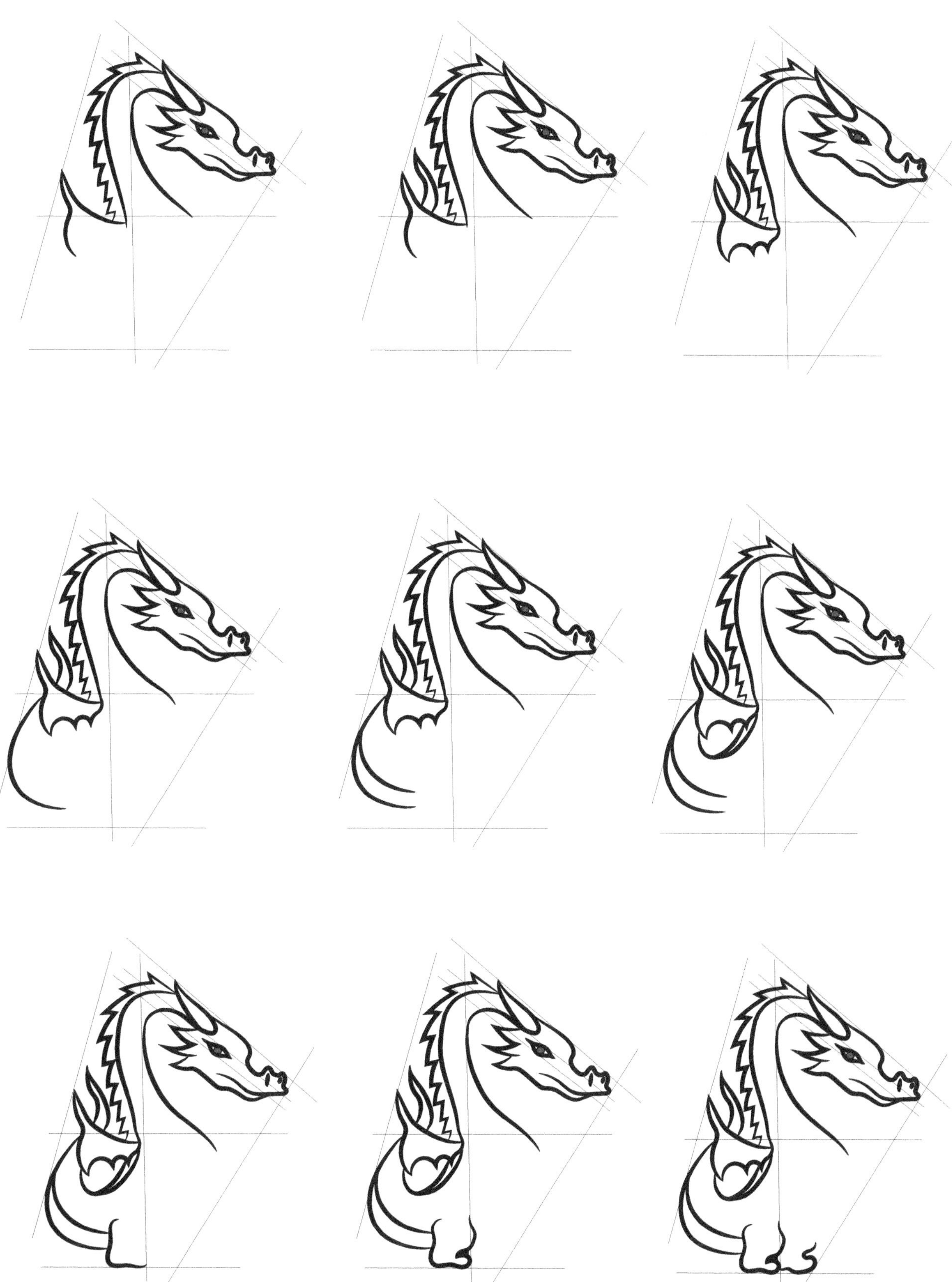

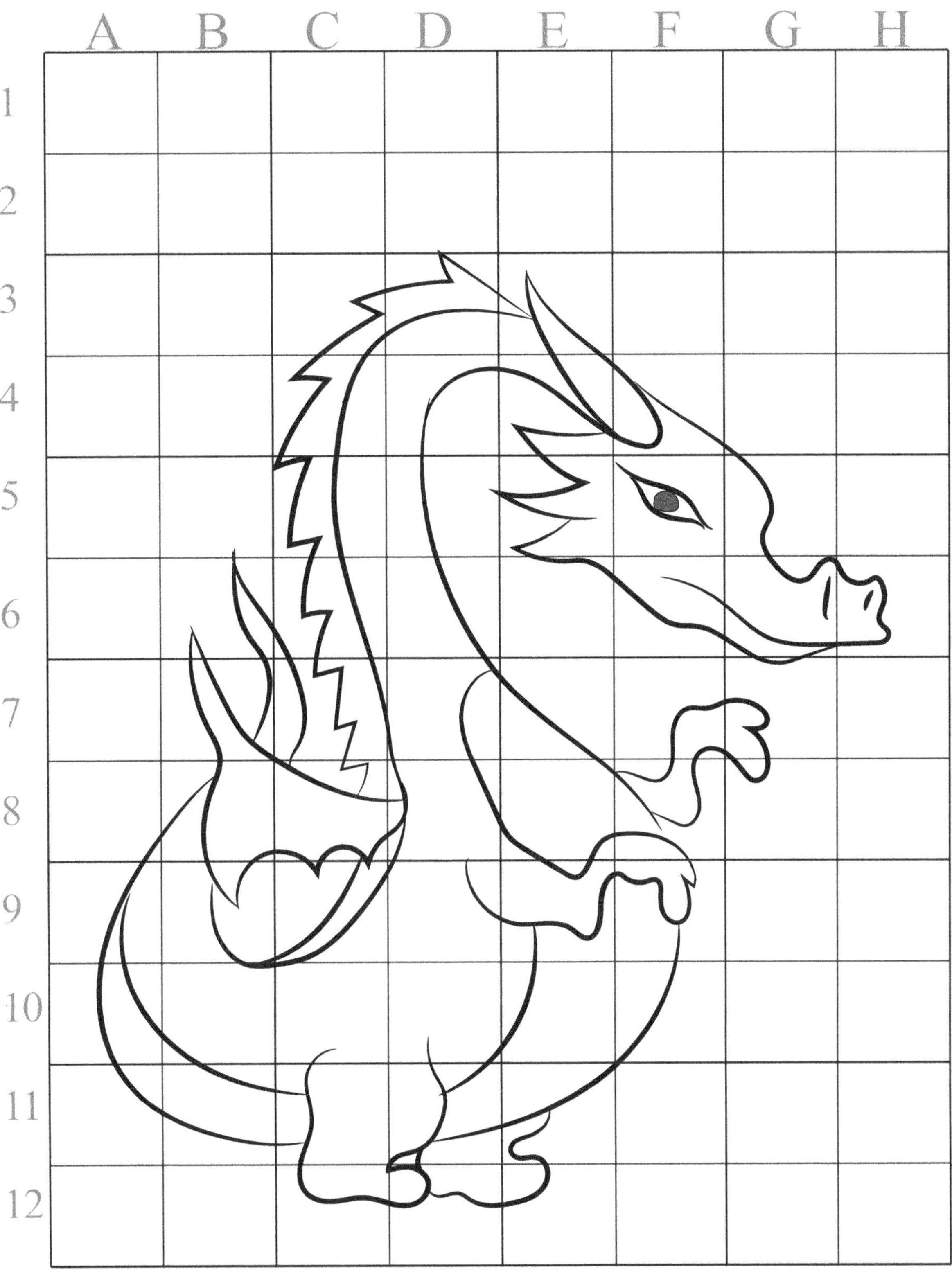

A B C D E F G H
1
2
3
4
5
6
7
8
9
10
11
12

9. Try changing your
character's features to
create alternative
versions.

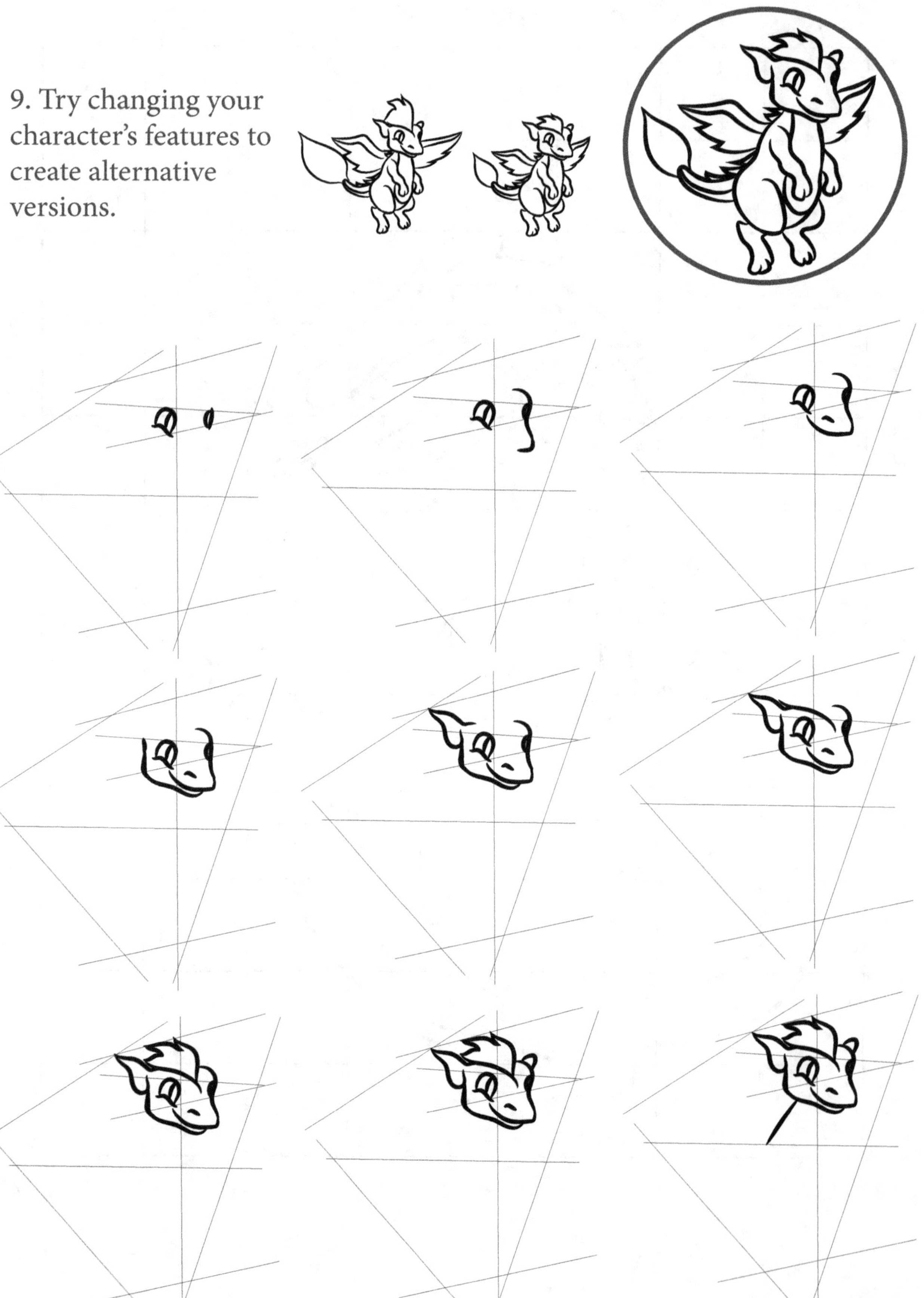

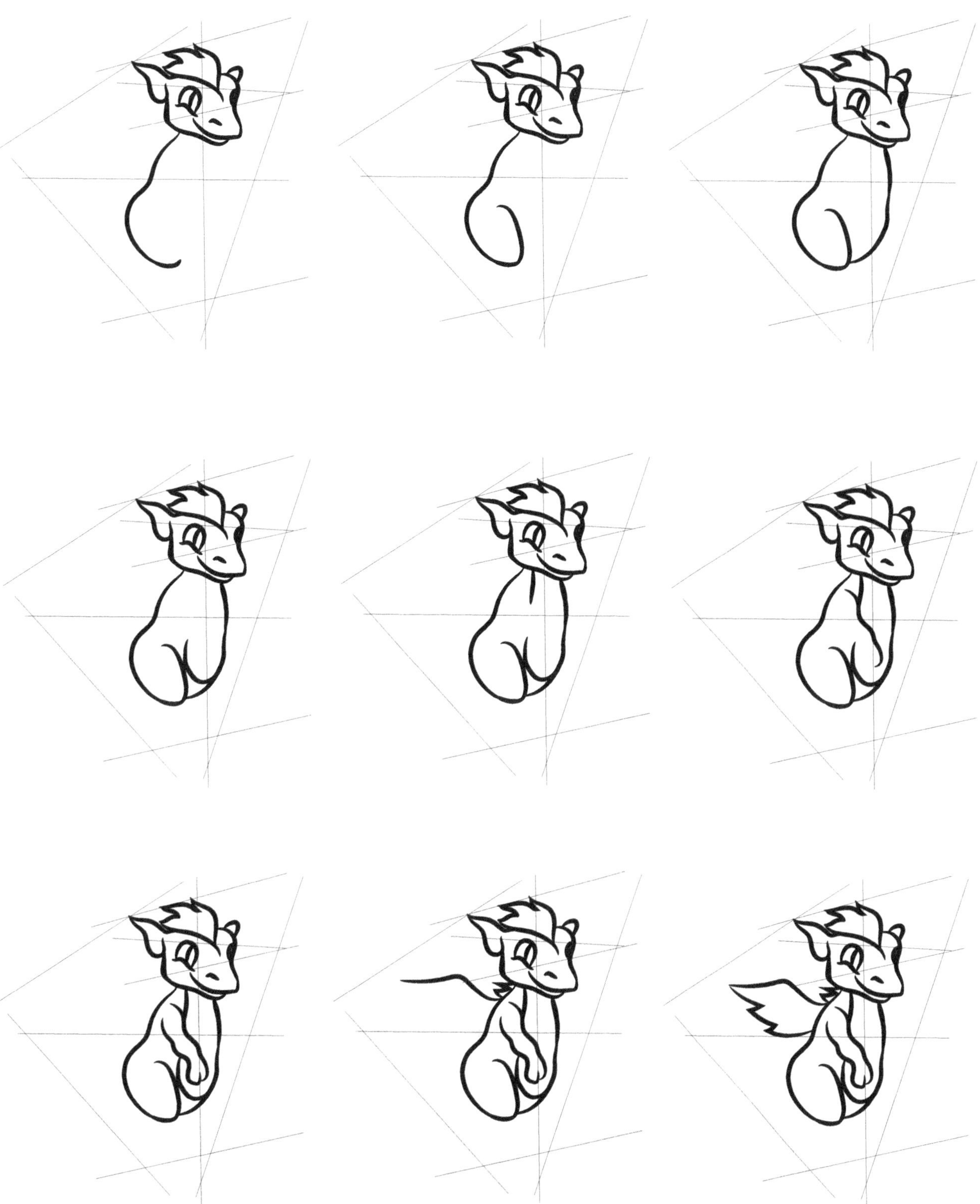

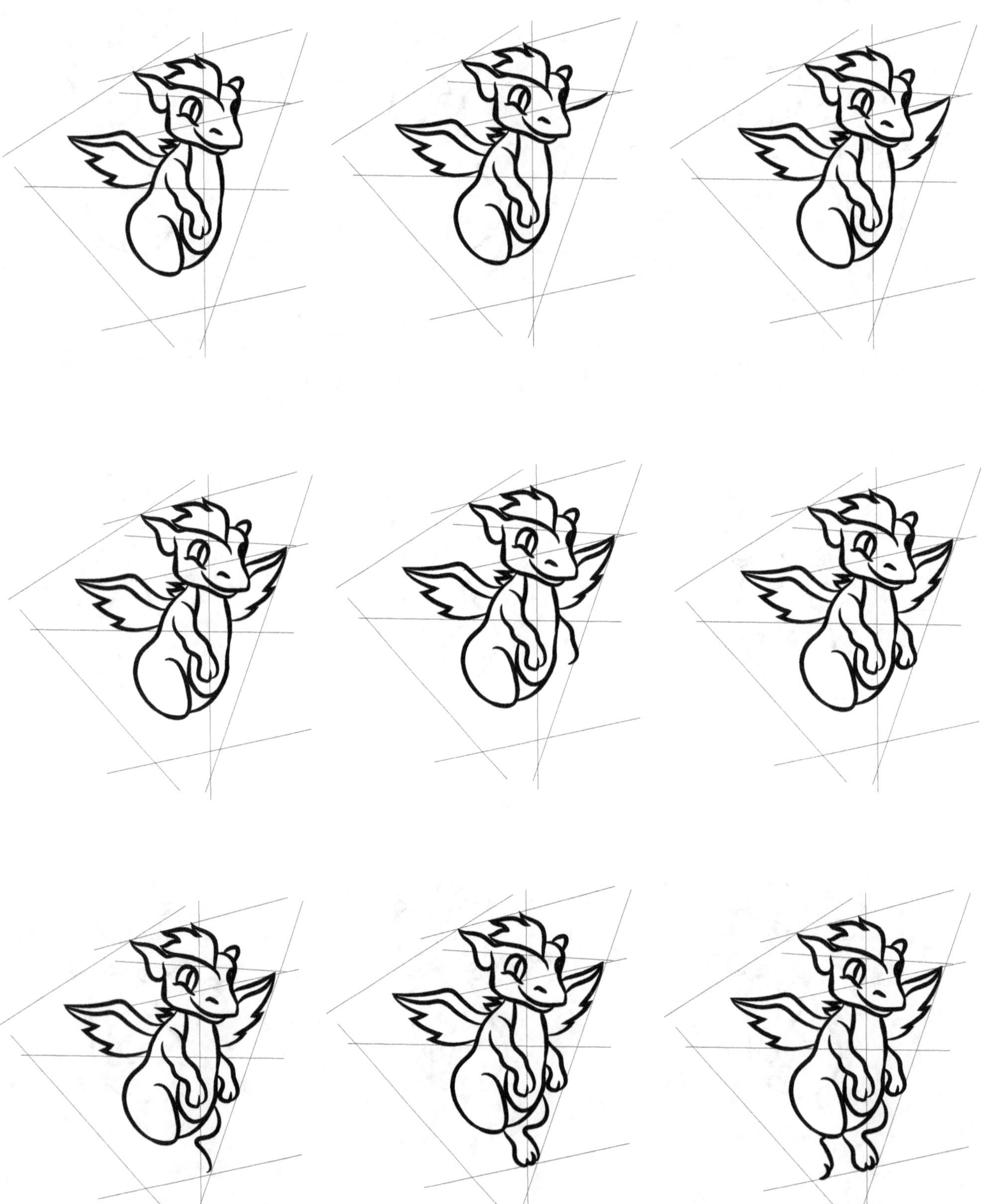

A B C D E F G H
1
2
3
4
5
6
7
8
9
10
11
12

10. Extend or reduce the width of your grid to make changes to your character.

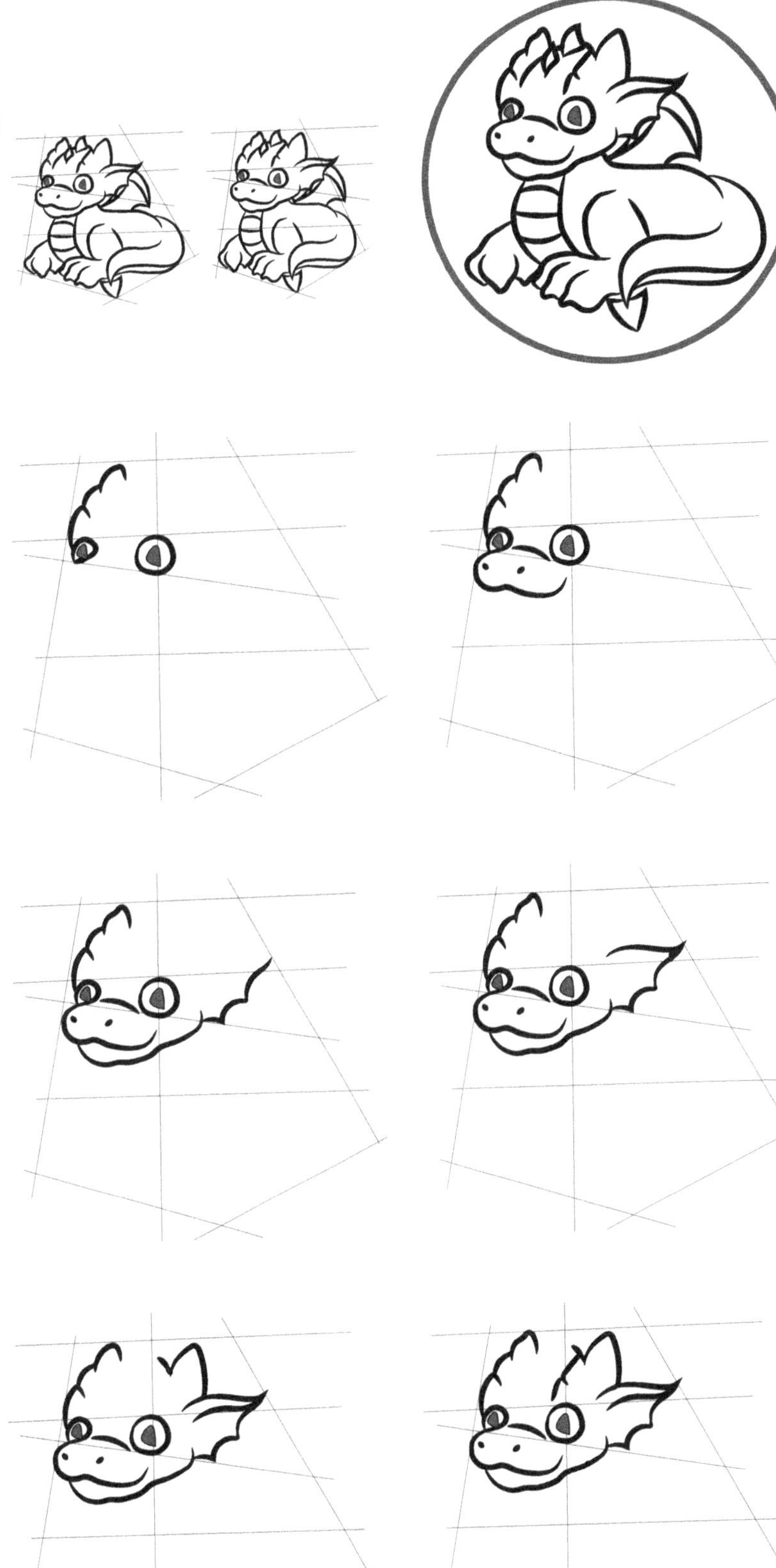

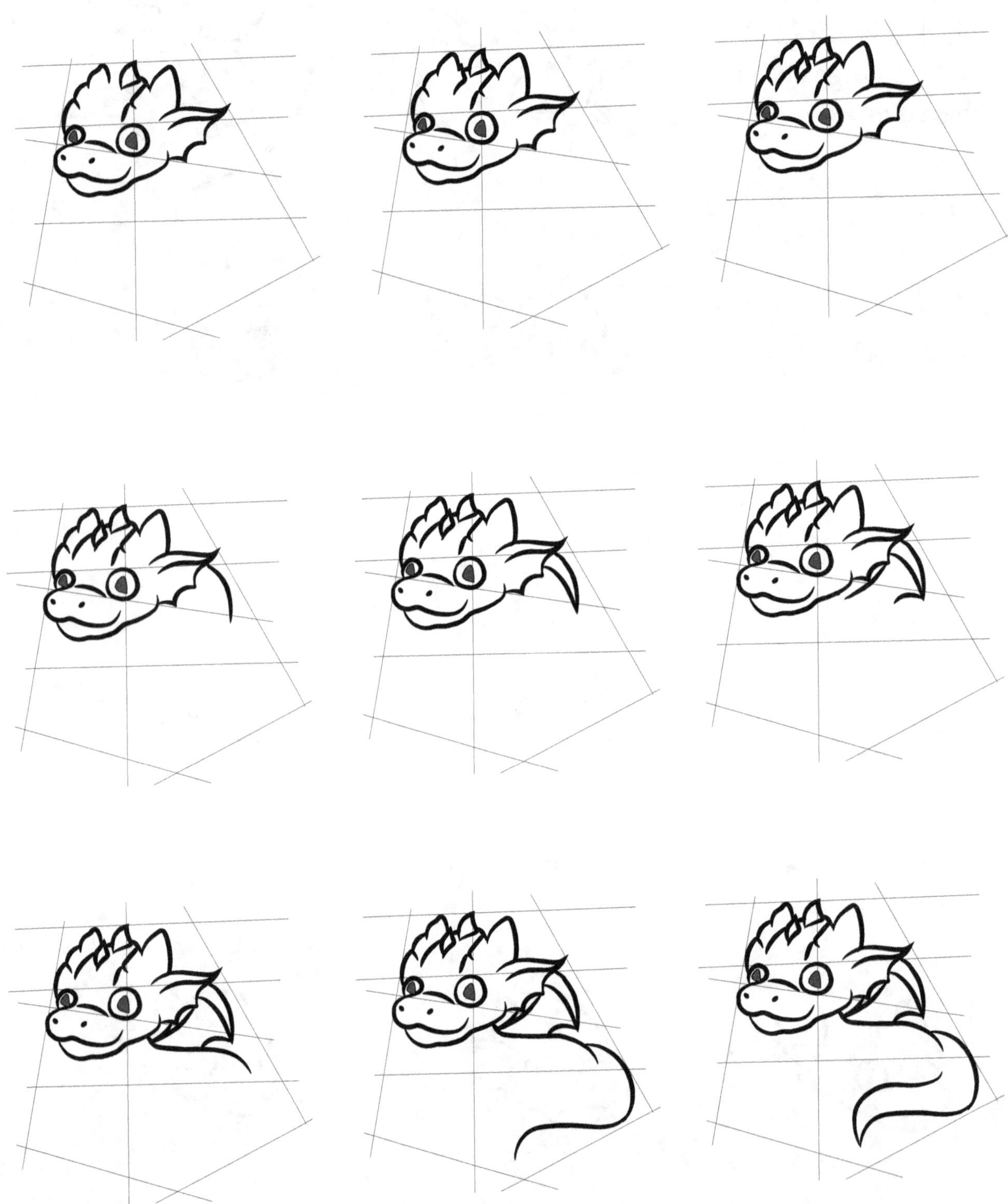

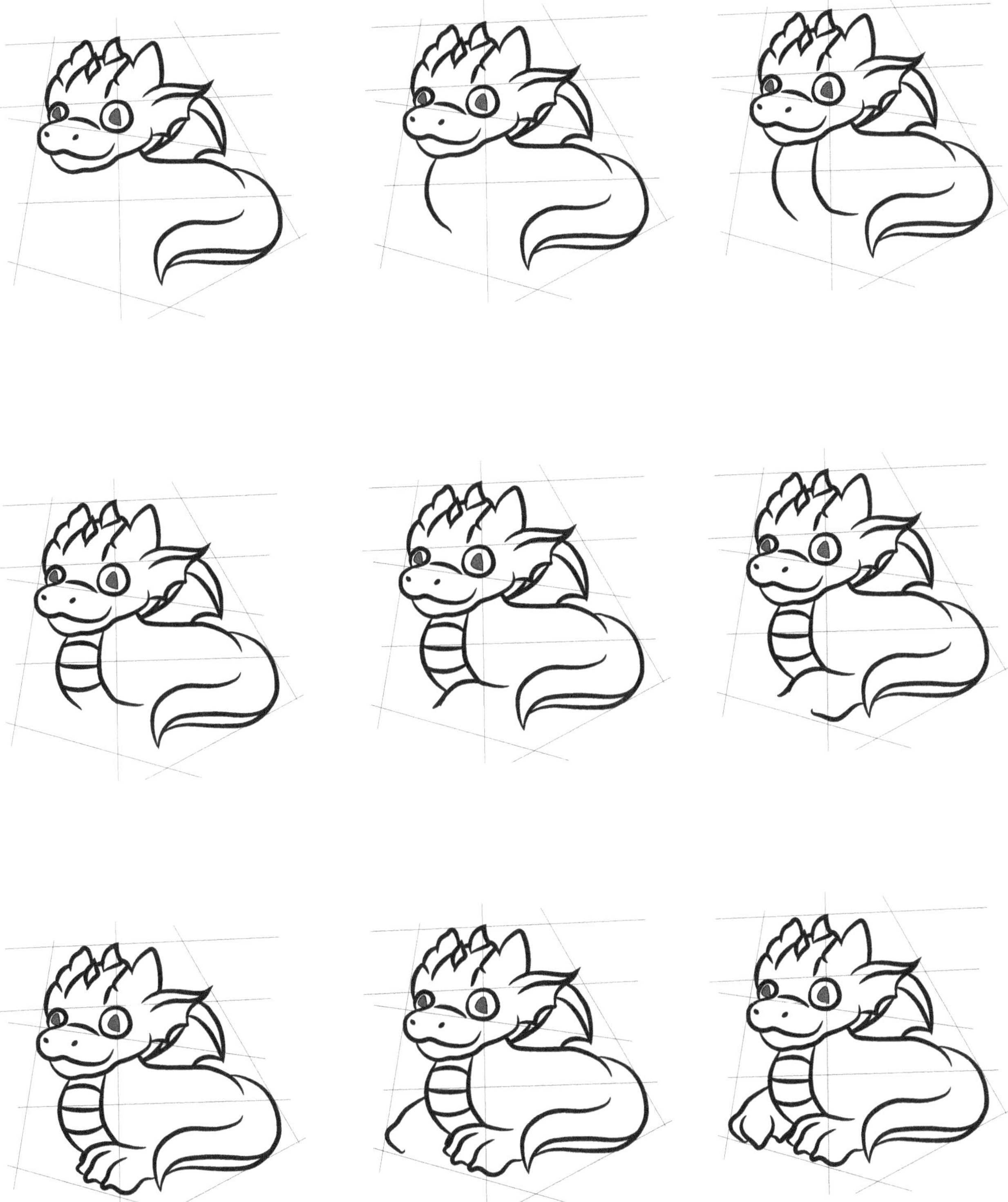

11. You can turn your character's head while keeping the position of its body the same.

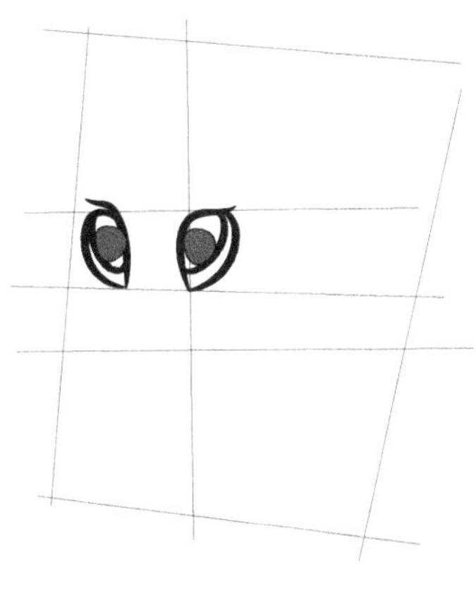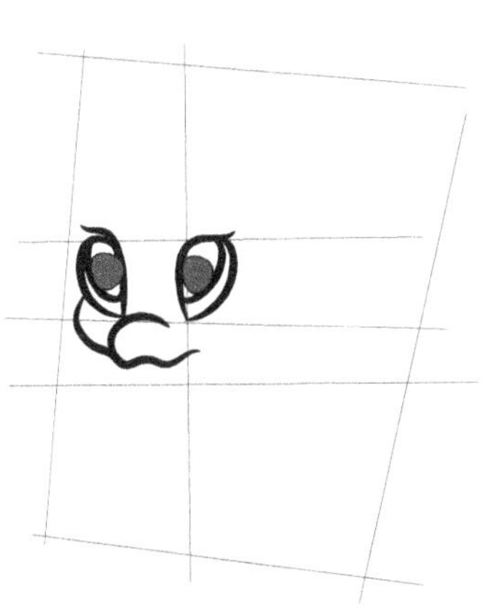

A B C D E F G H
1
2
3
4
5
6
7
8
9
10
11
12

12. Add extra
features to your
character to make it
look more original.

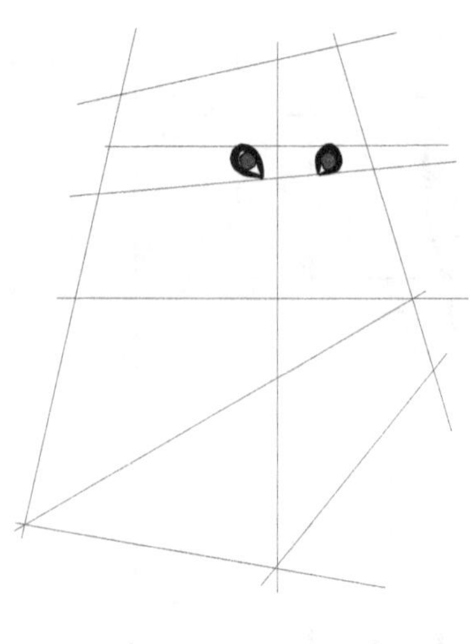 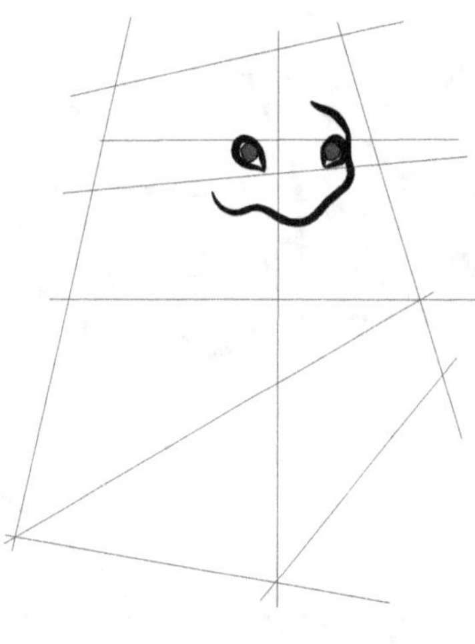 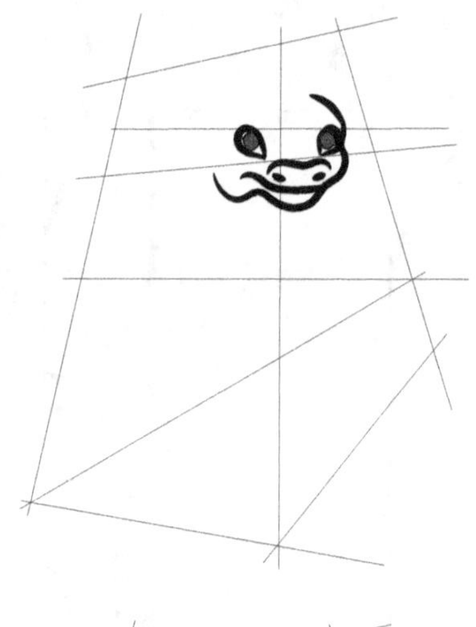

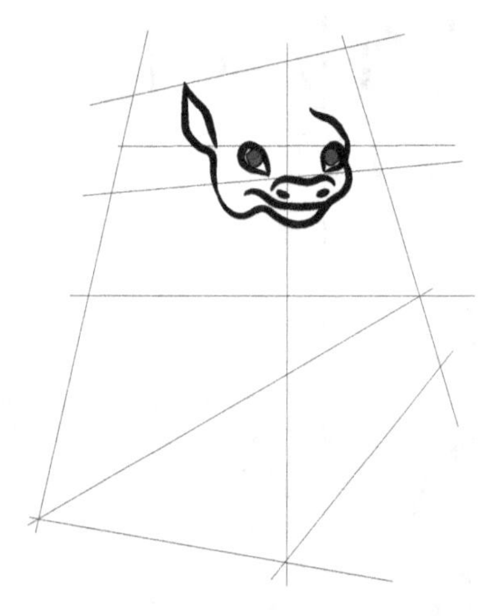 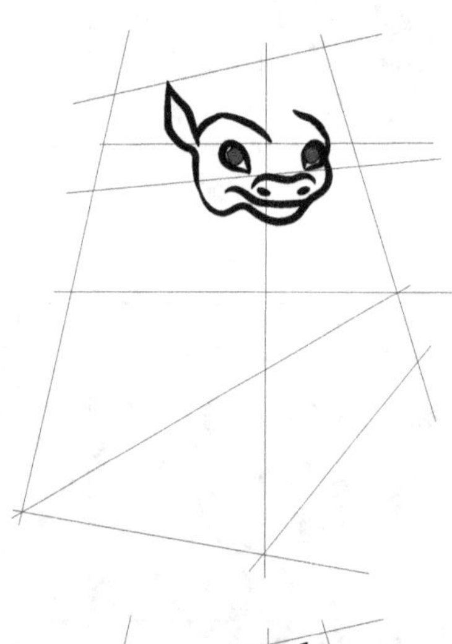 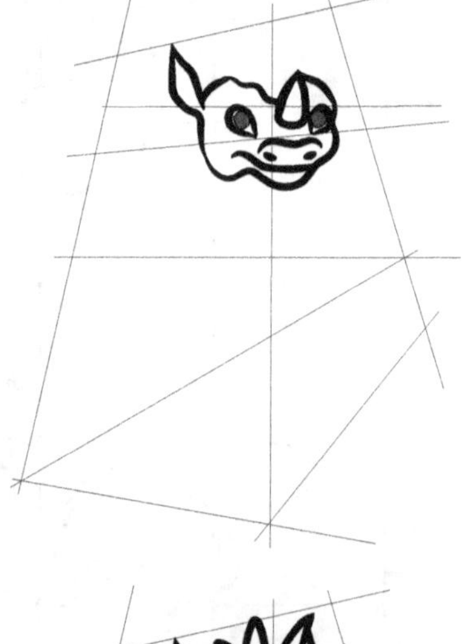

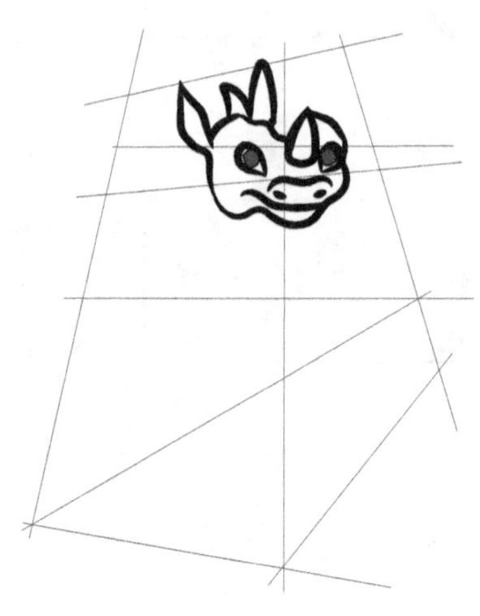  

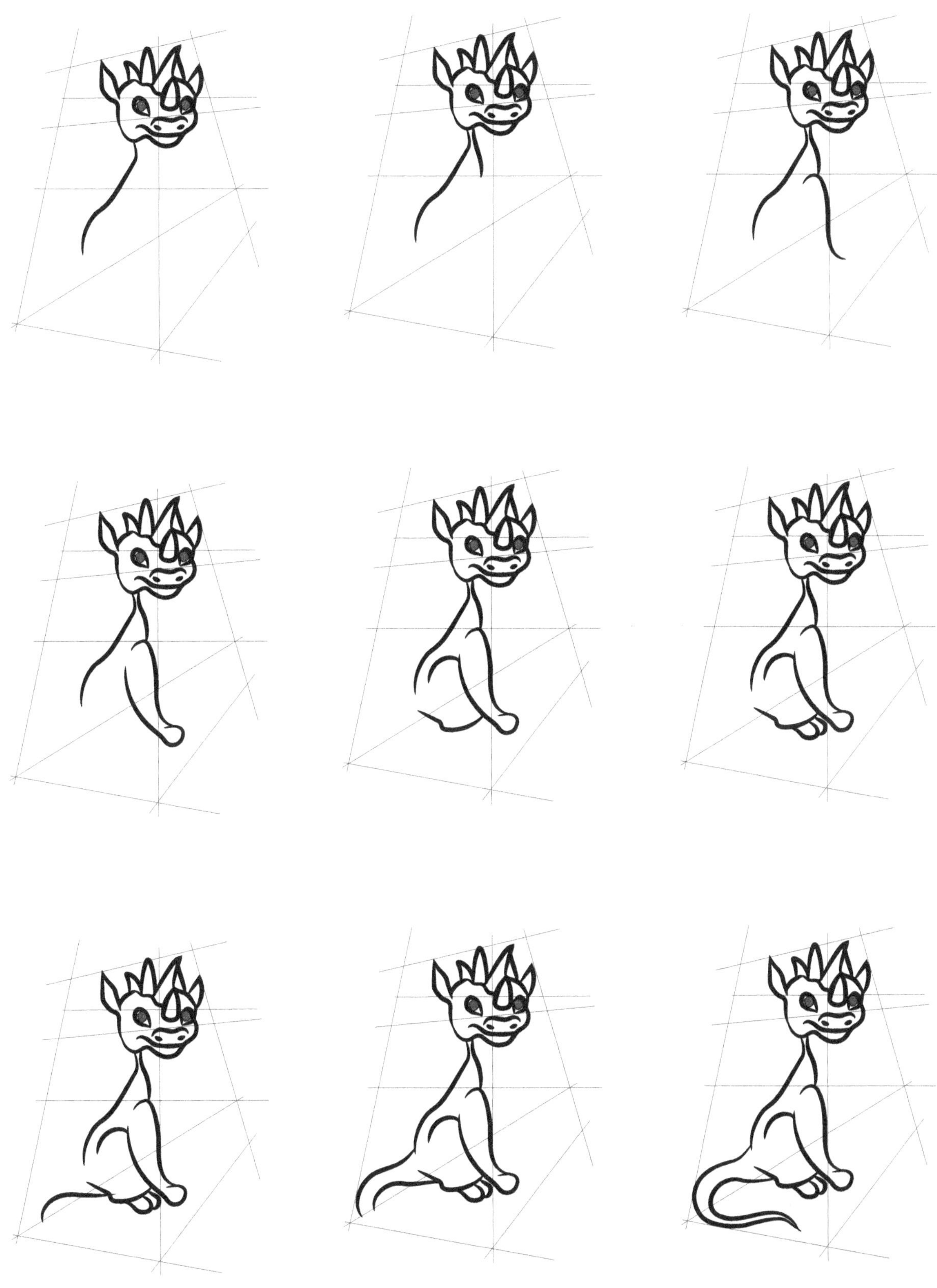

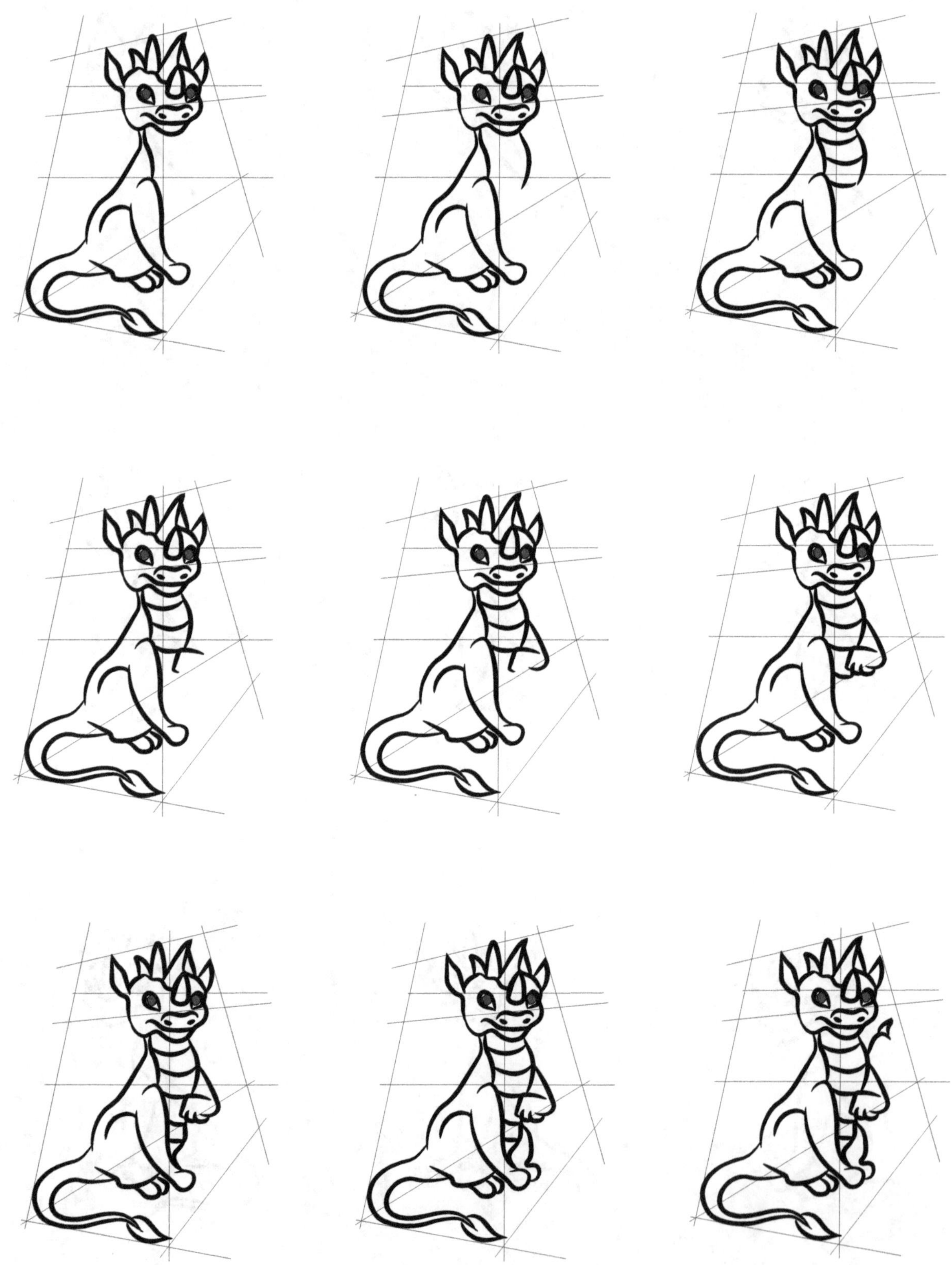

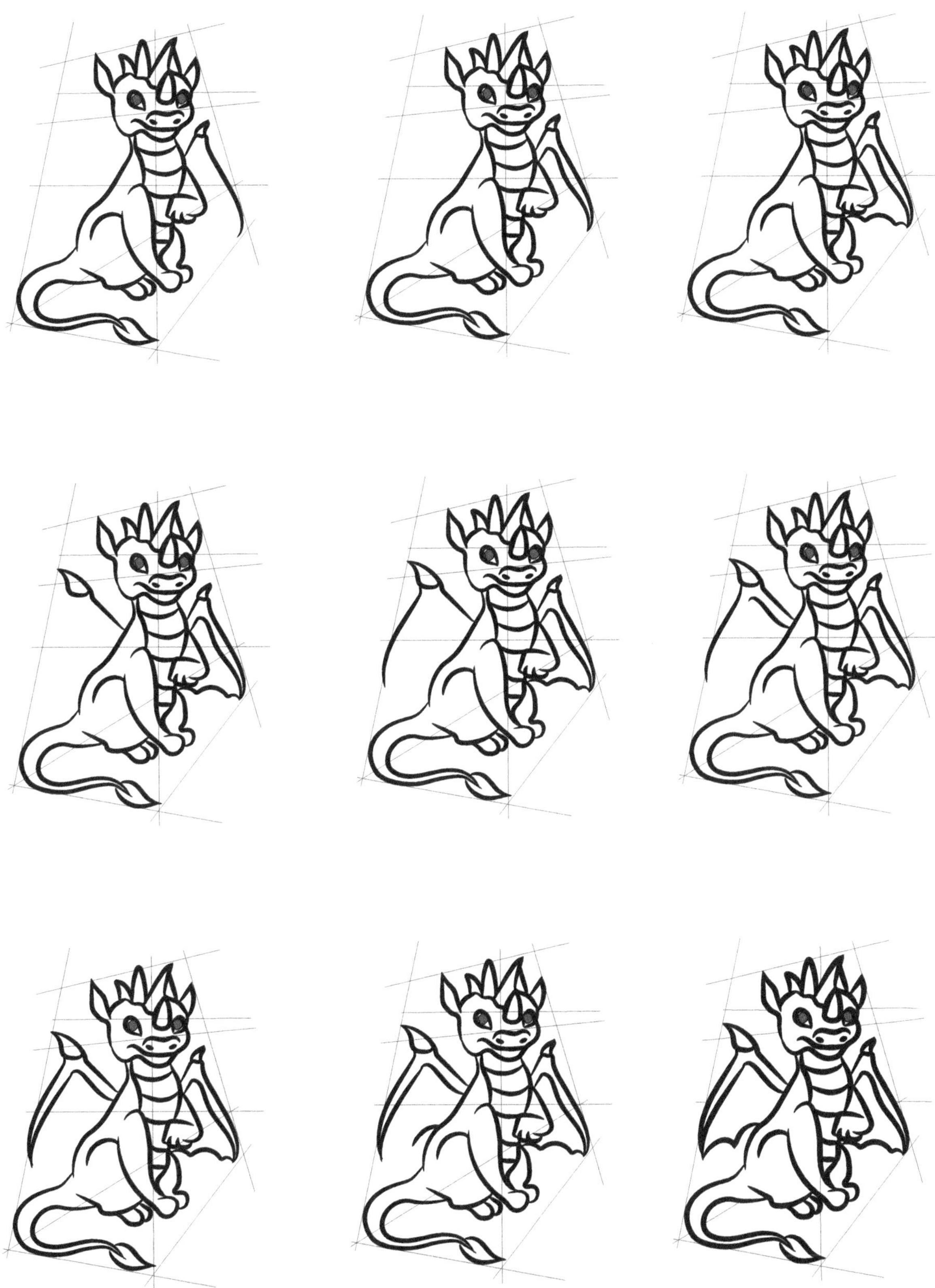

A B C D E F G H
1
2
3
4
5
6
7
8
9
10
11
12

13. The use of ellipses in grids can be very helpful when you want to create round shapes.

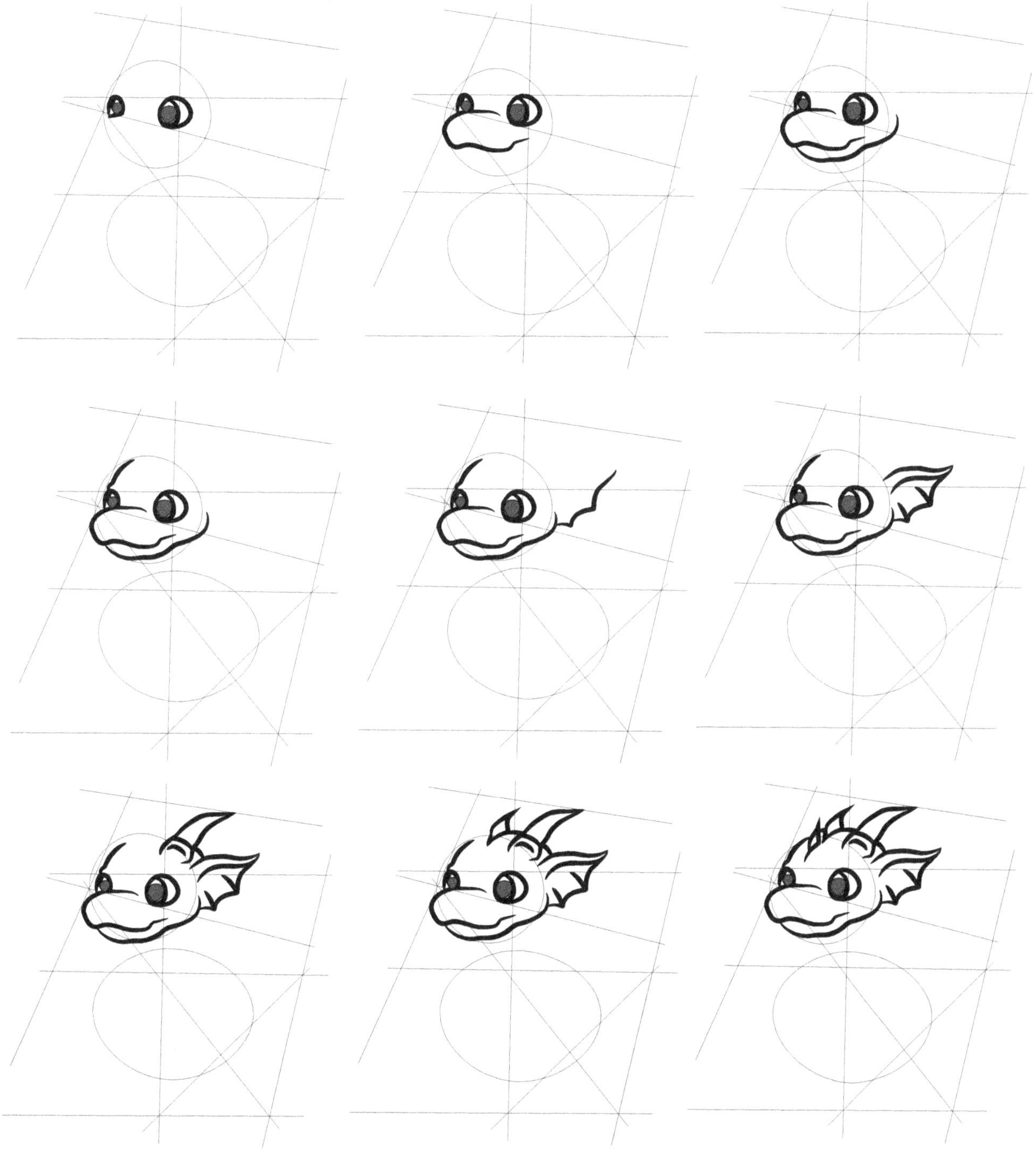

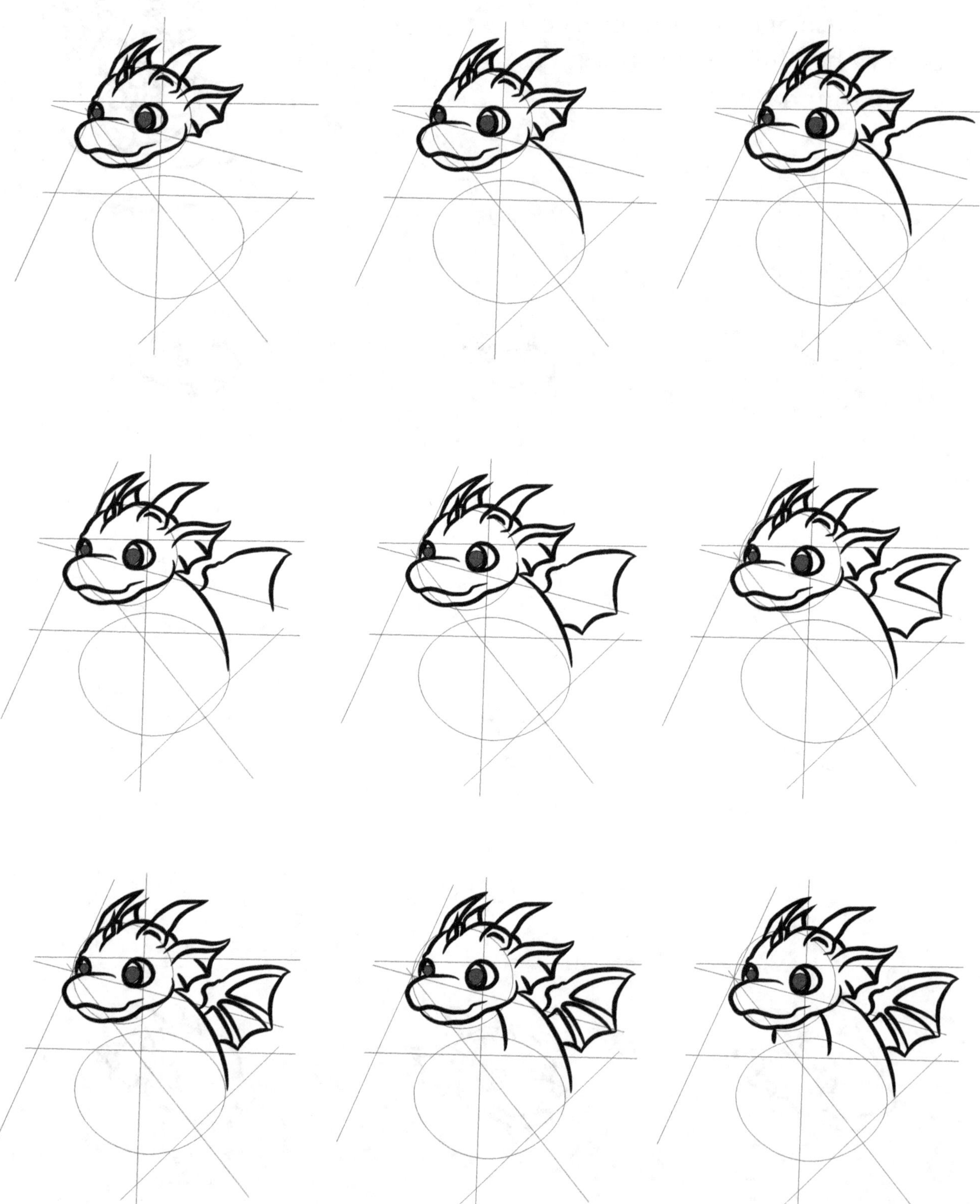

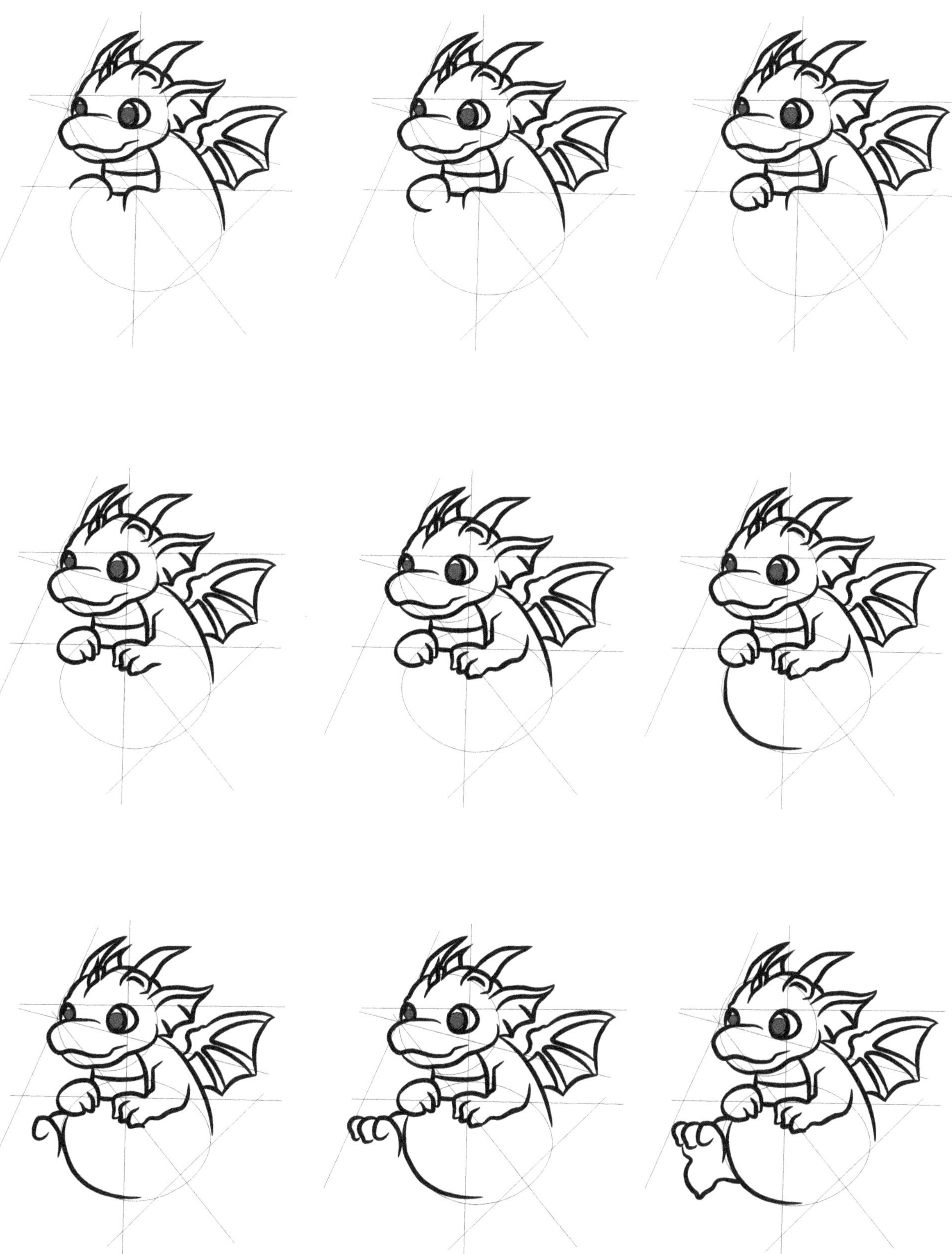

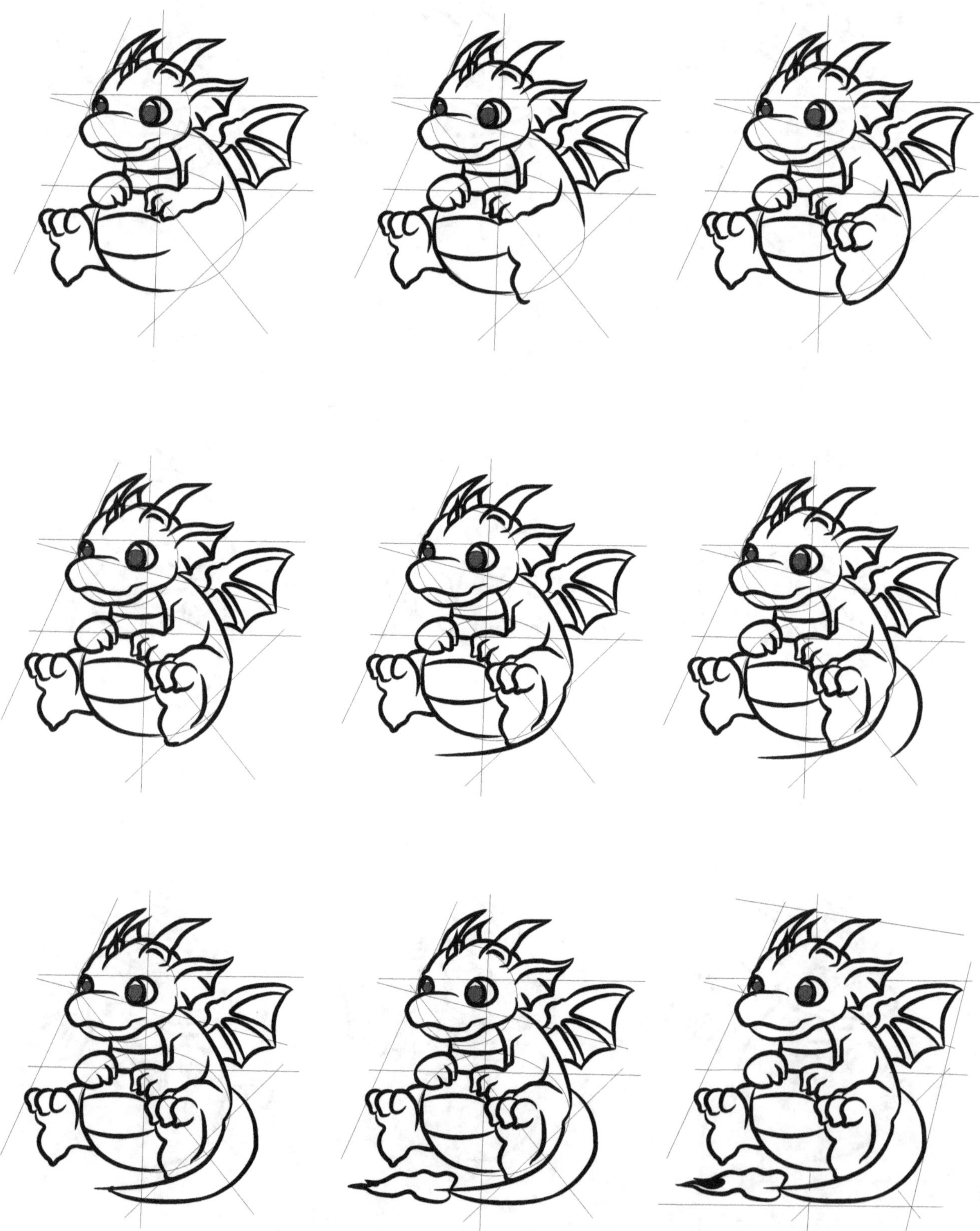

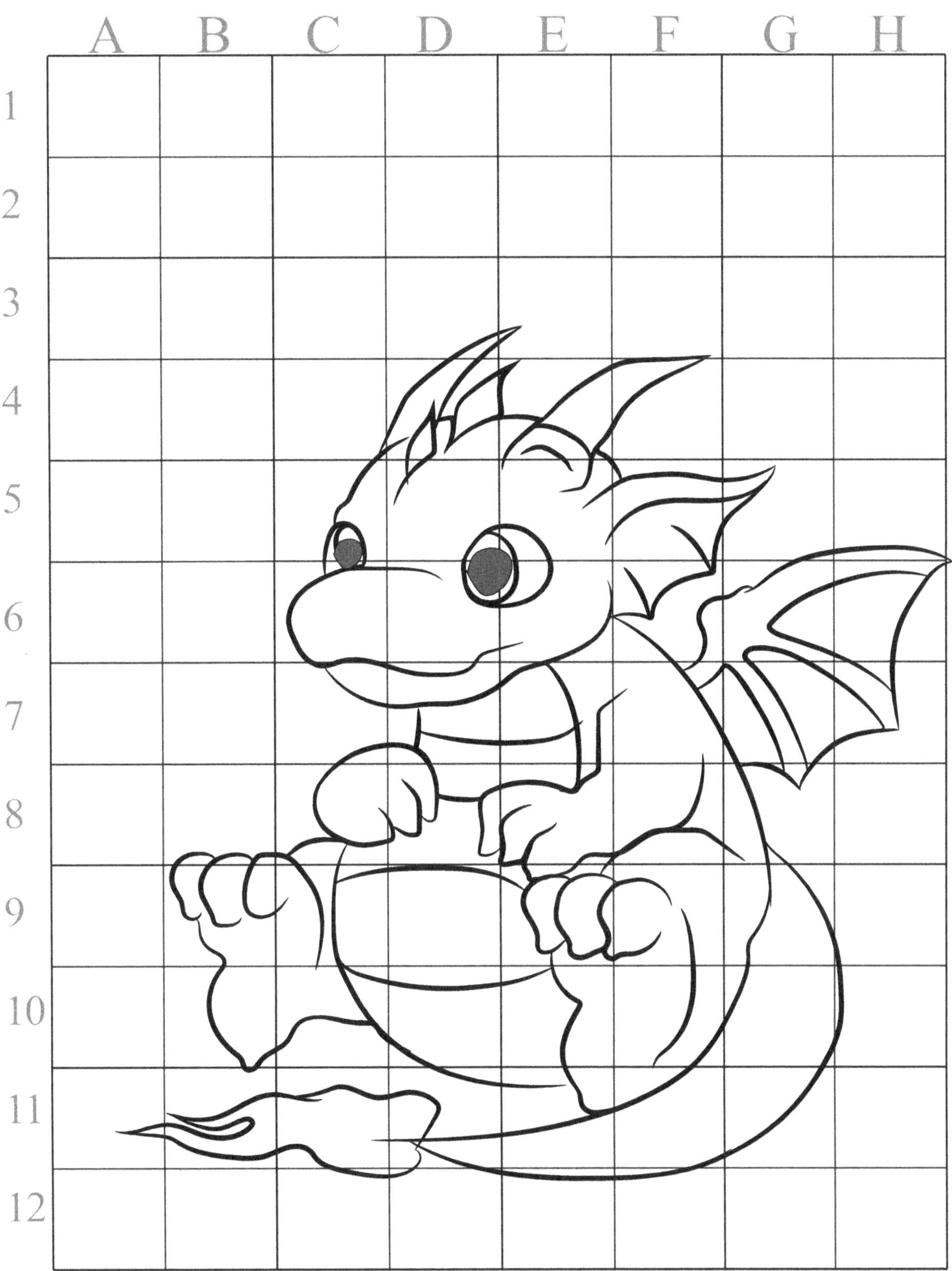

A B C D E F G H
1
2
3
4
5
6
7
8
9
10
11
12

14. When starting a more complex
drawing it is best to think of it as a lot
of small parts. Focusing on one small
part at a time will make your project
feel less overwhelming.

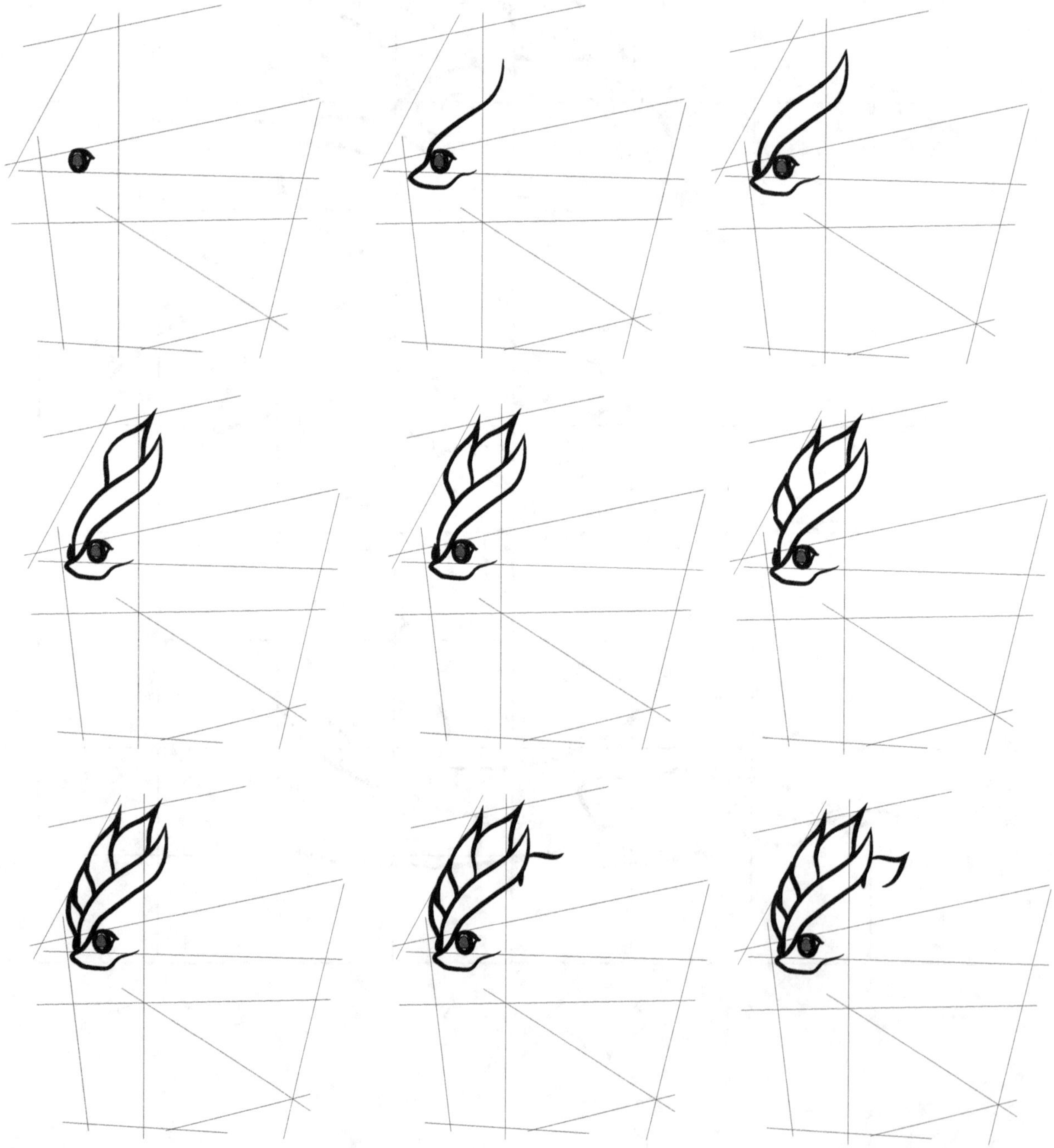

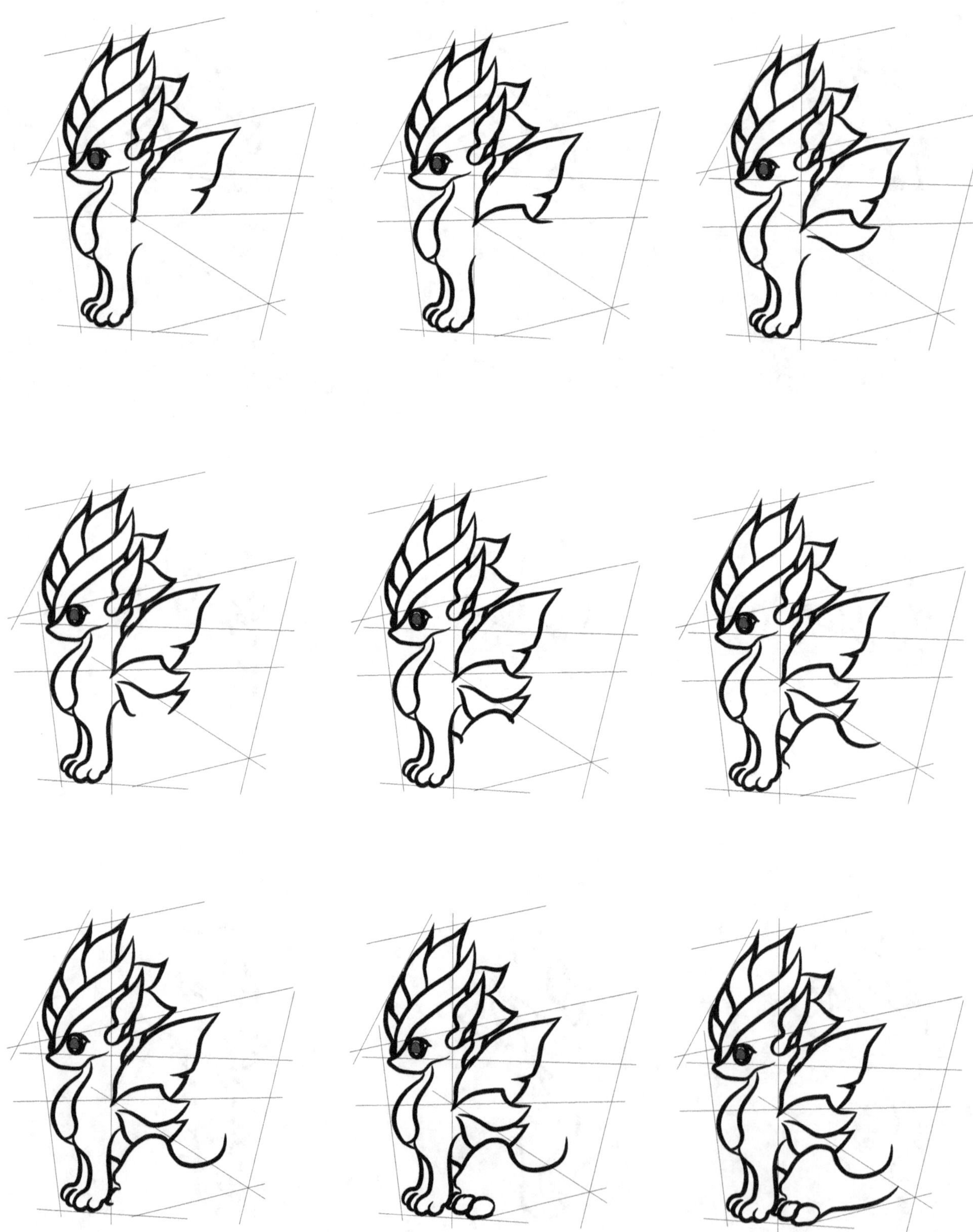

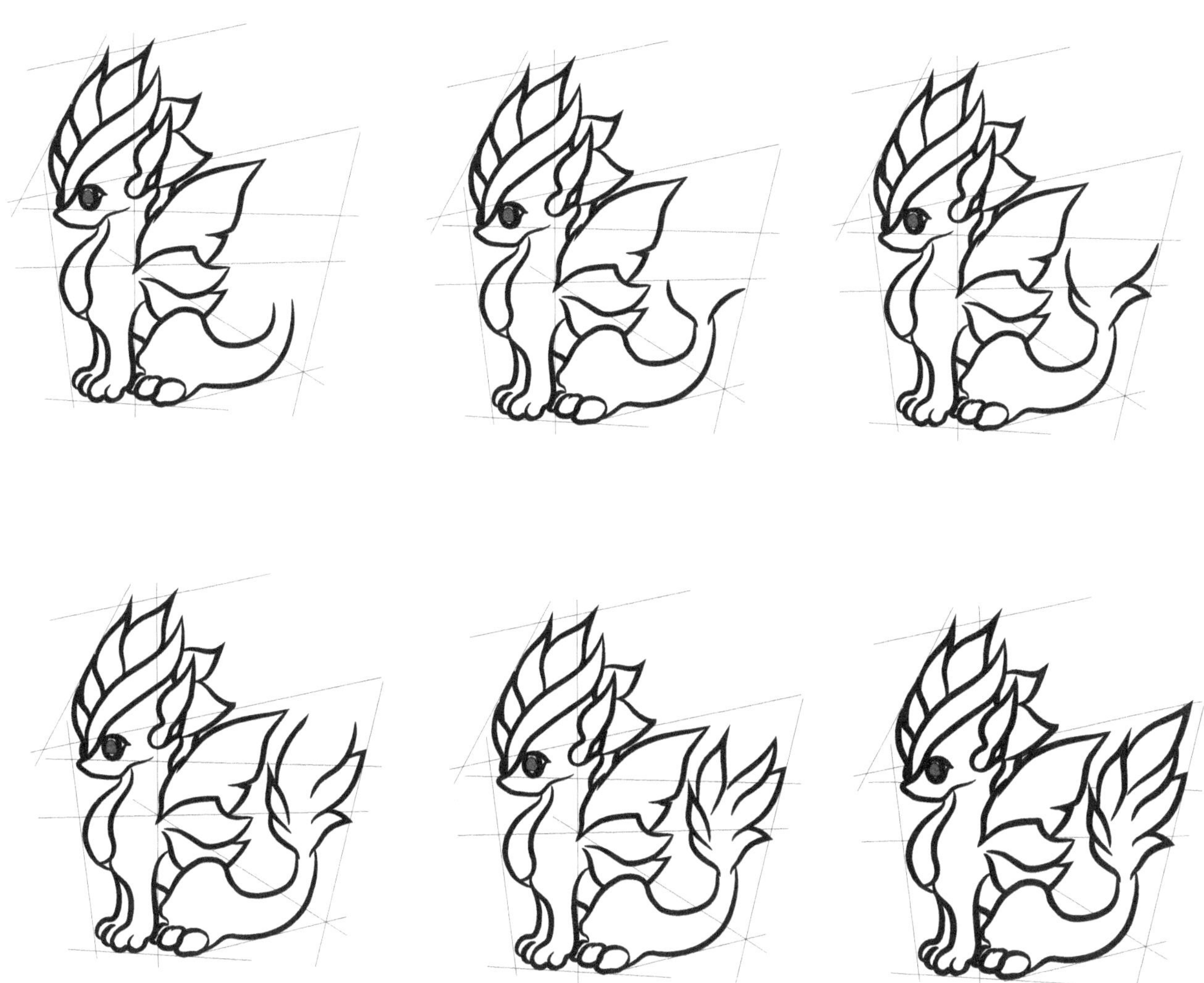

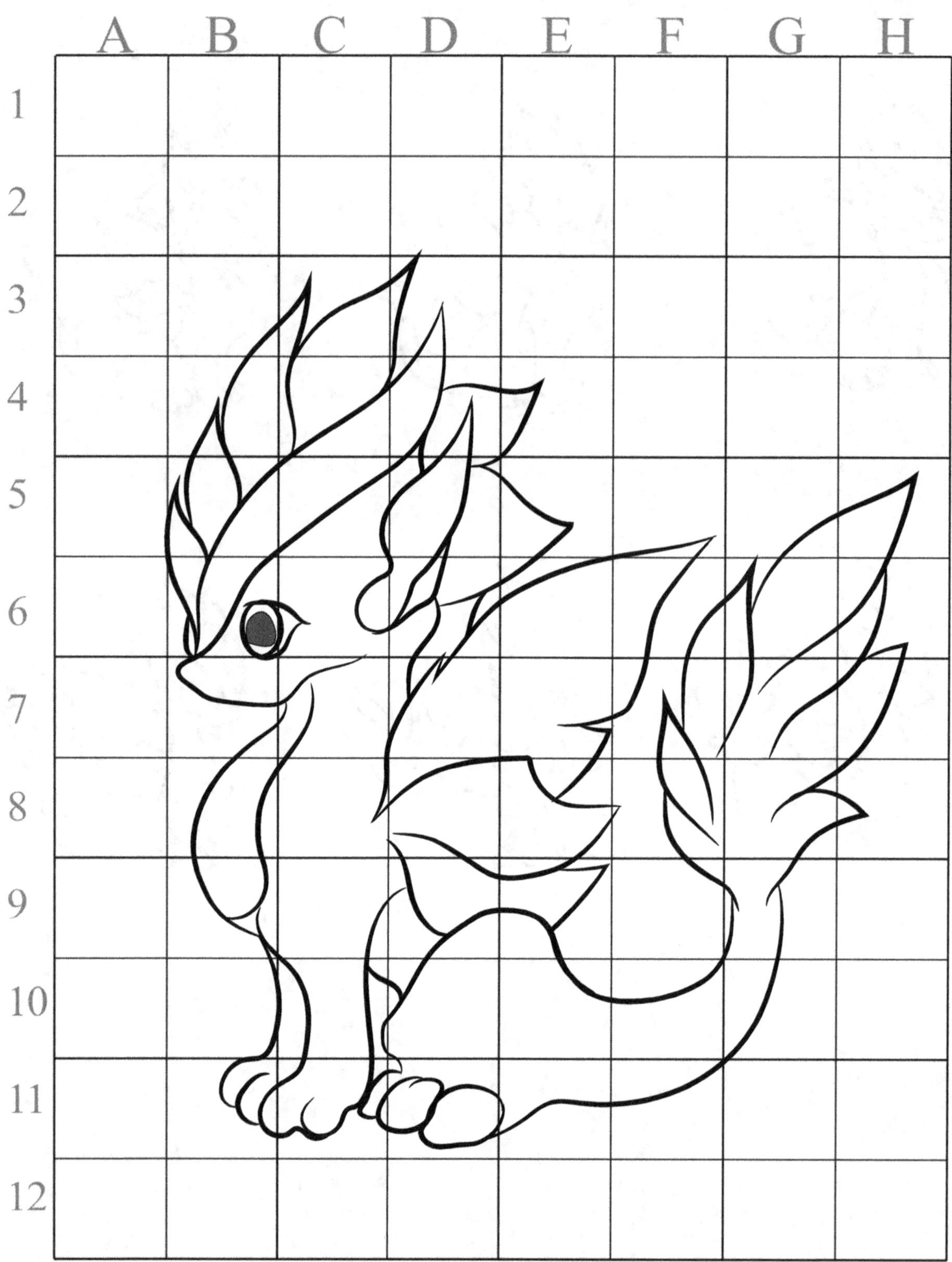

15. The positioning of an arm and a hand can make a big difference. In this drawing the hand position indicates that the character is thinking about something.

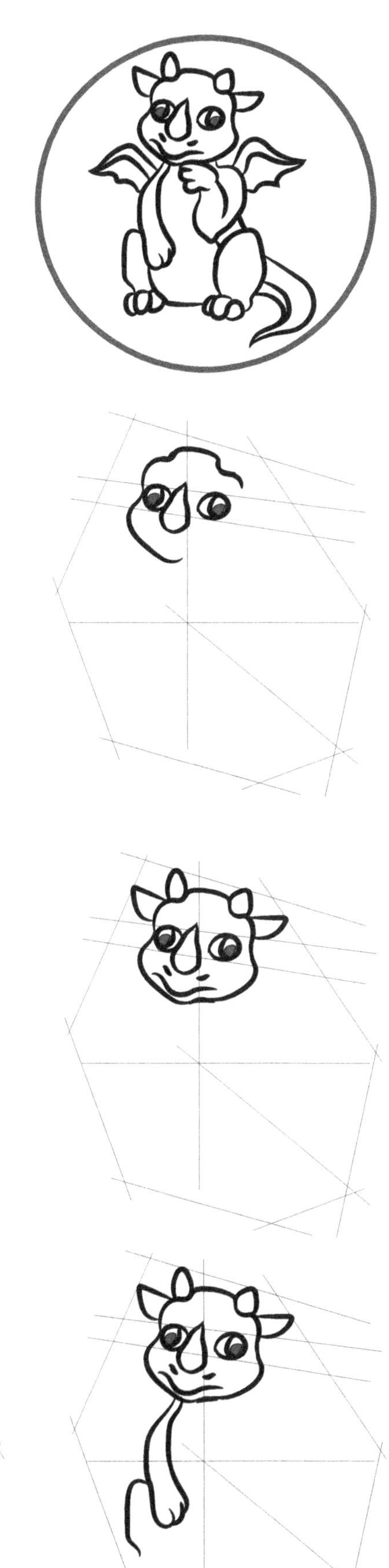

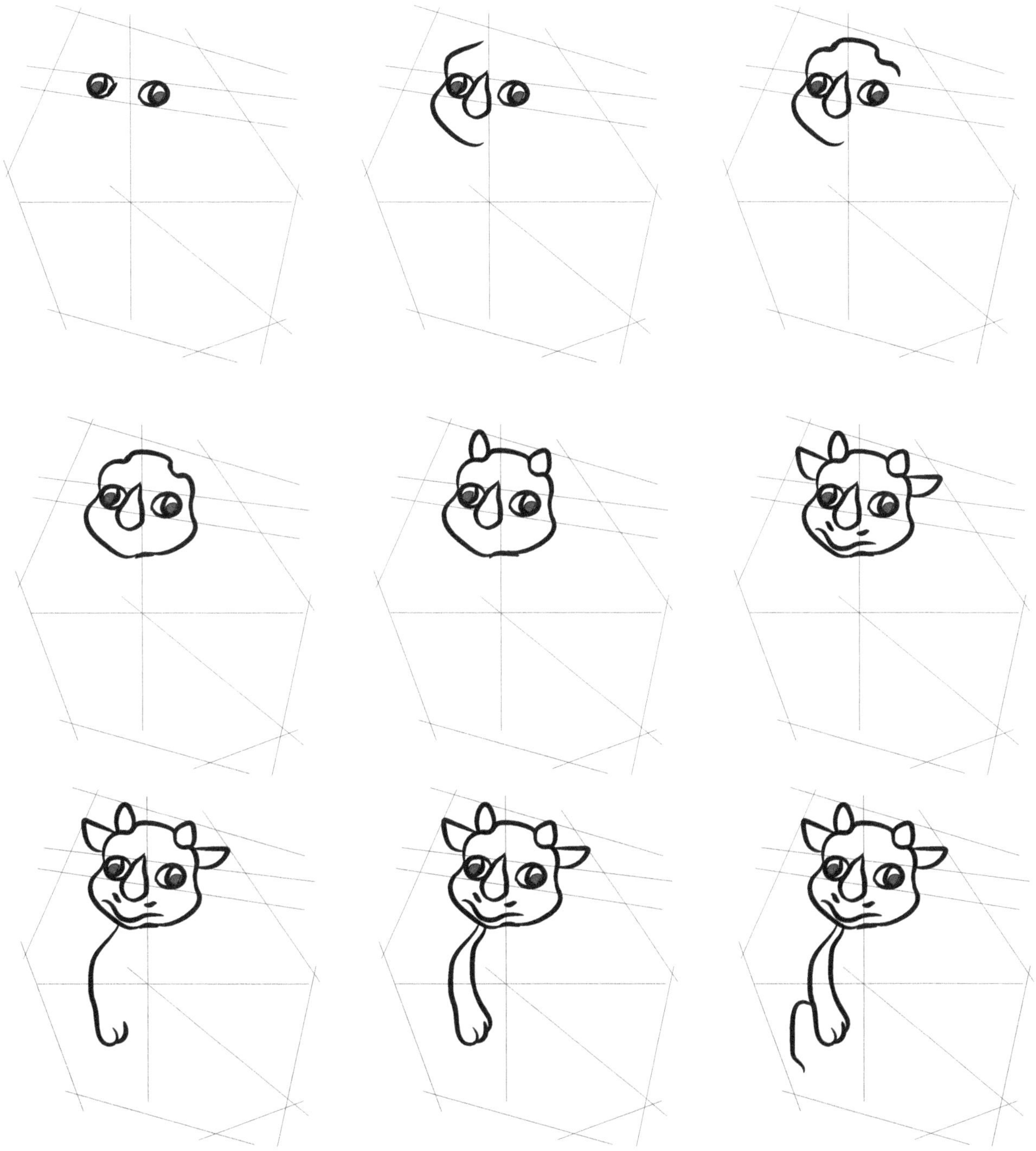

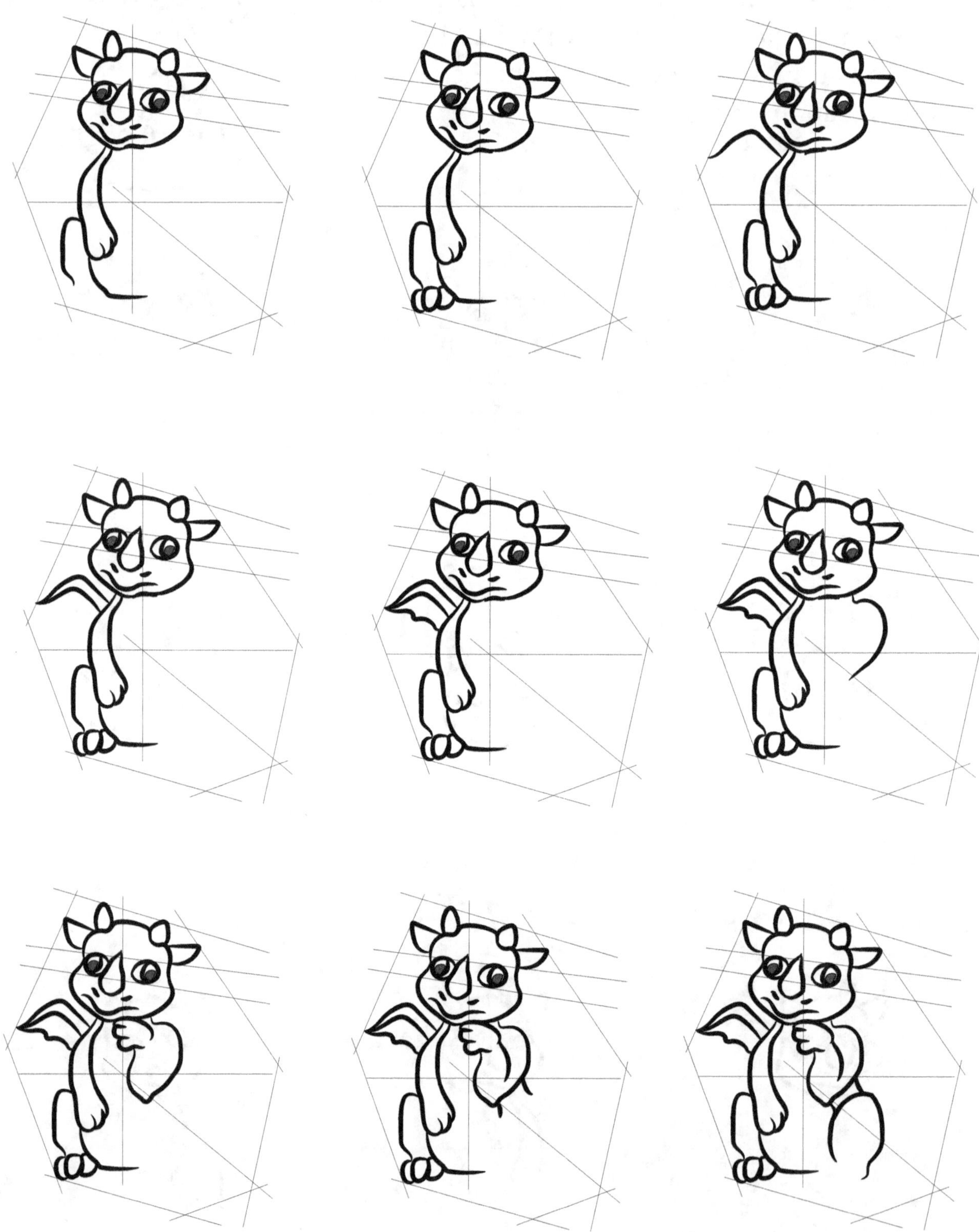

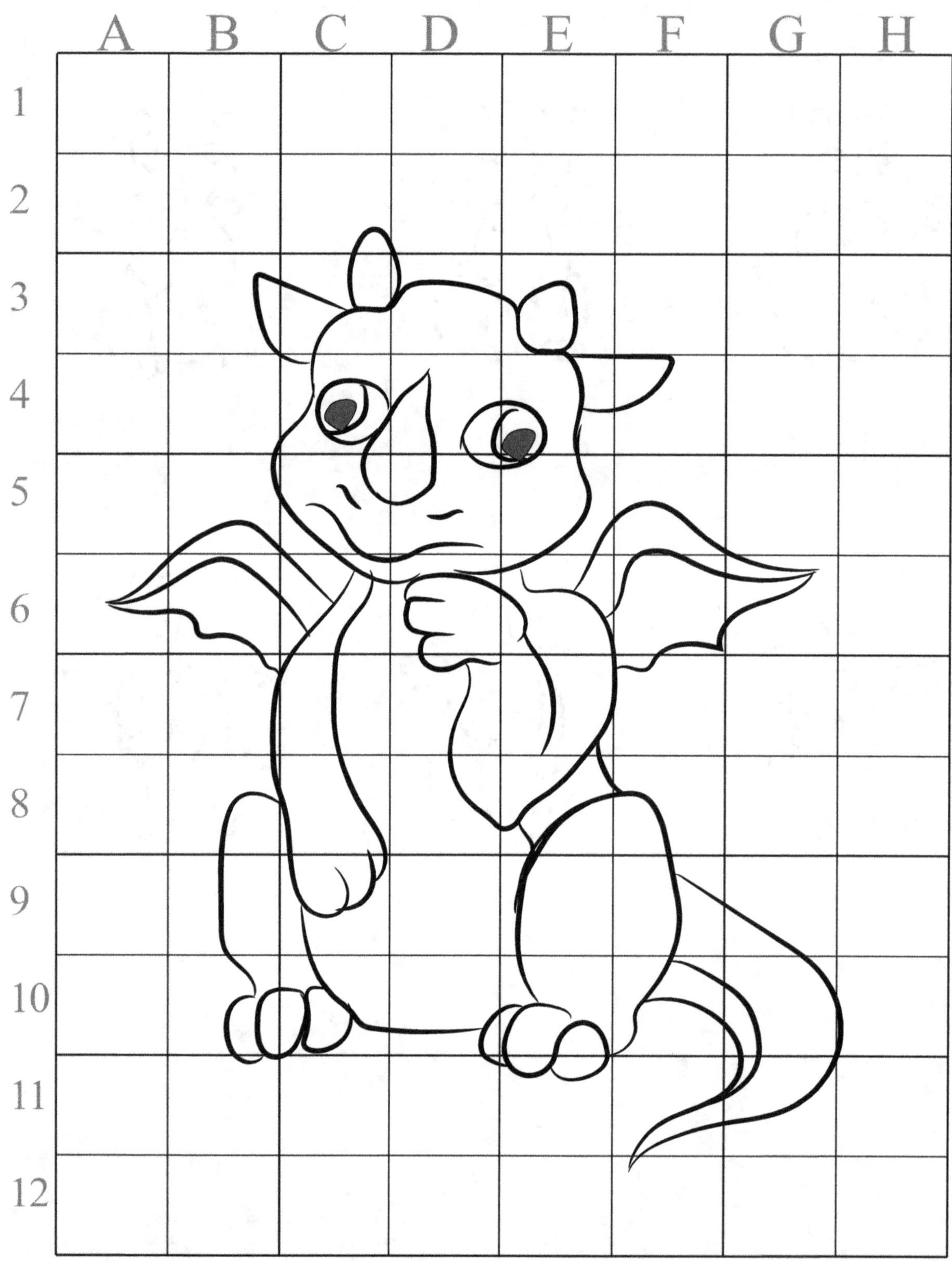

A B C D E F G H
1
2
3
4
5
6
7
8
9
10
11
12

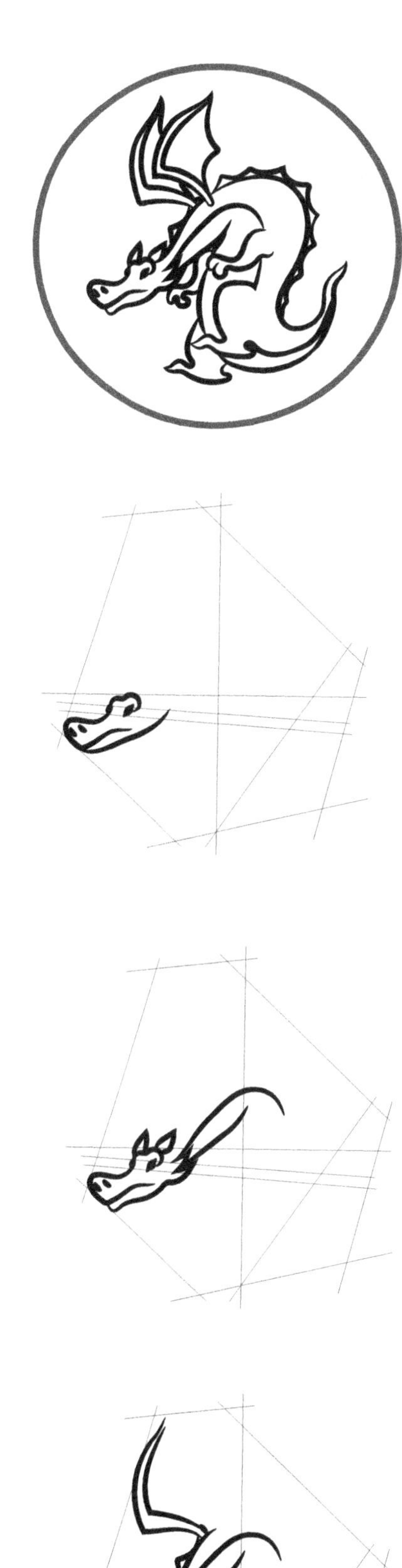

16. The wing size of this dragon compared with its body size suggests that it will not be able to fly. Luckily, no one has told this to dragon who can fly without any difficulty.

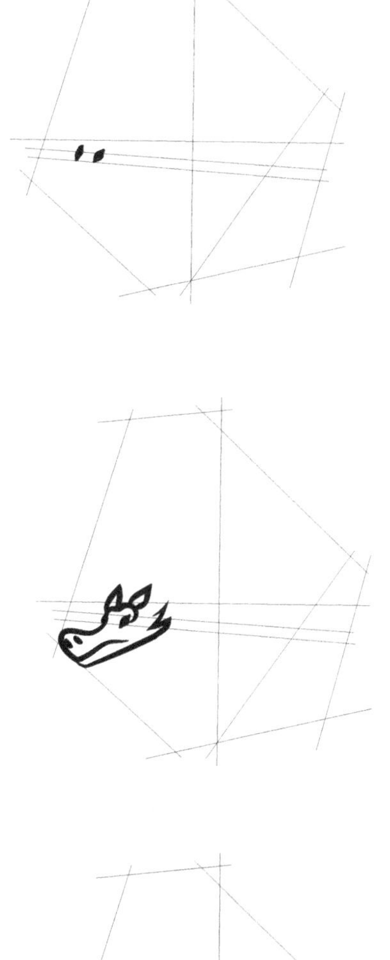

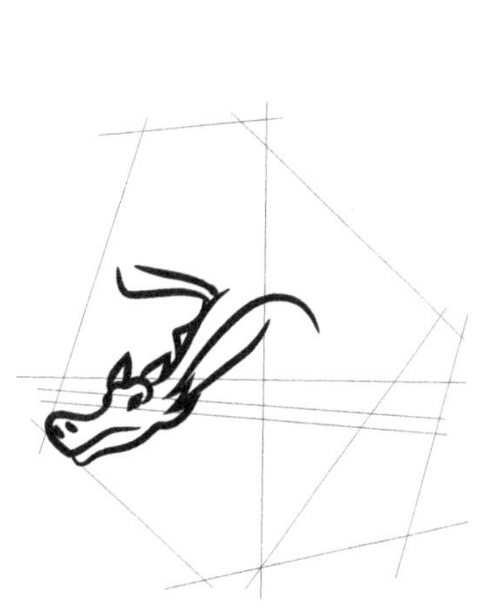

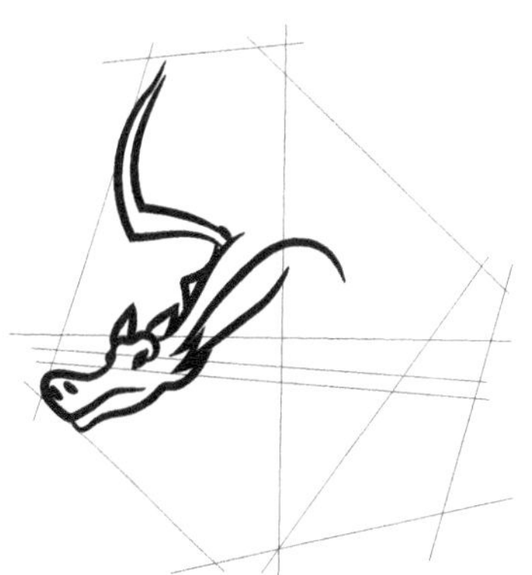

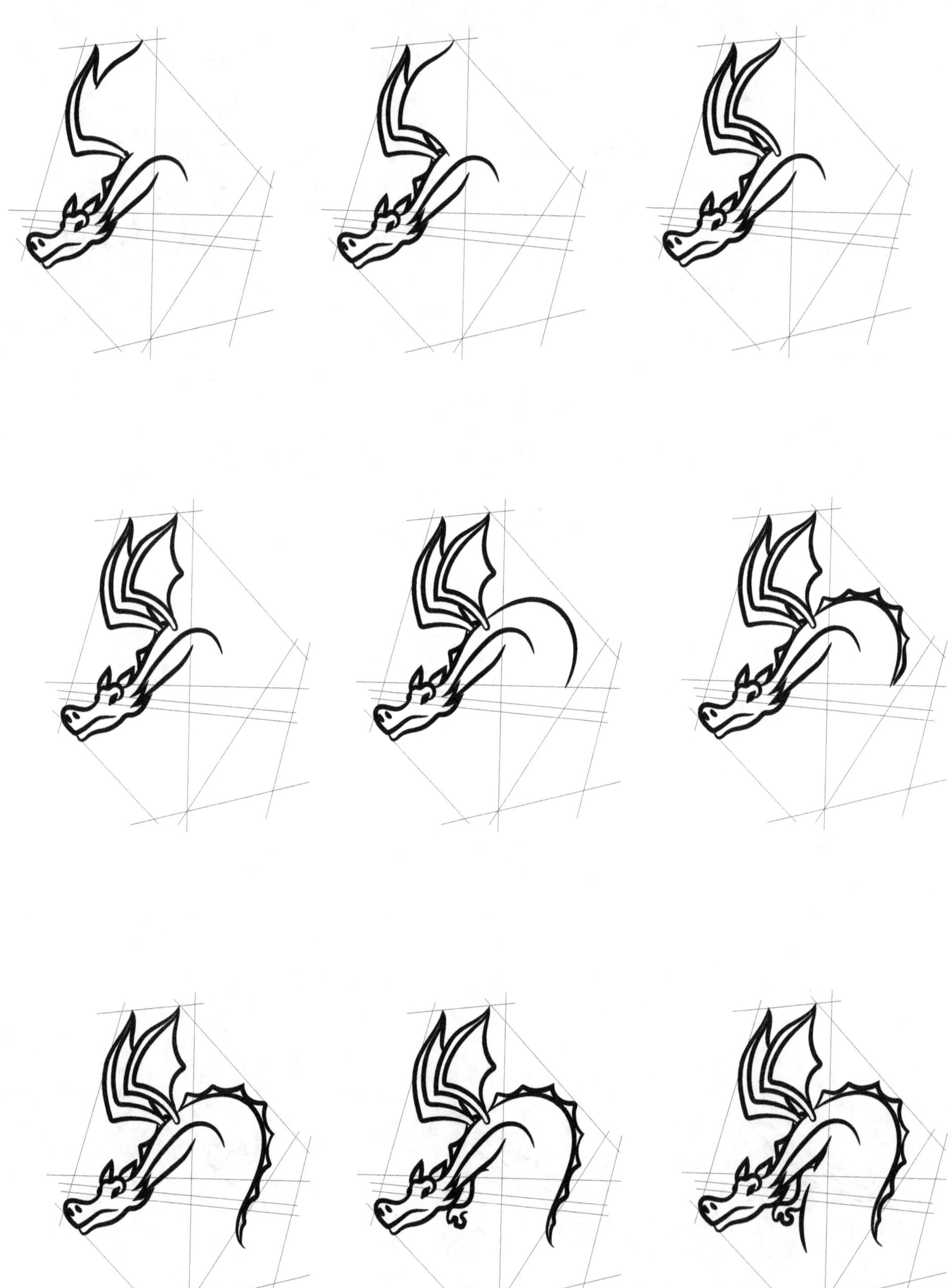

A B C D E F G H
1
2
3
4
5
6
7
8
9
10
11
12

17. You can make your character more
cartoon like by exaggerating its features.

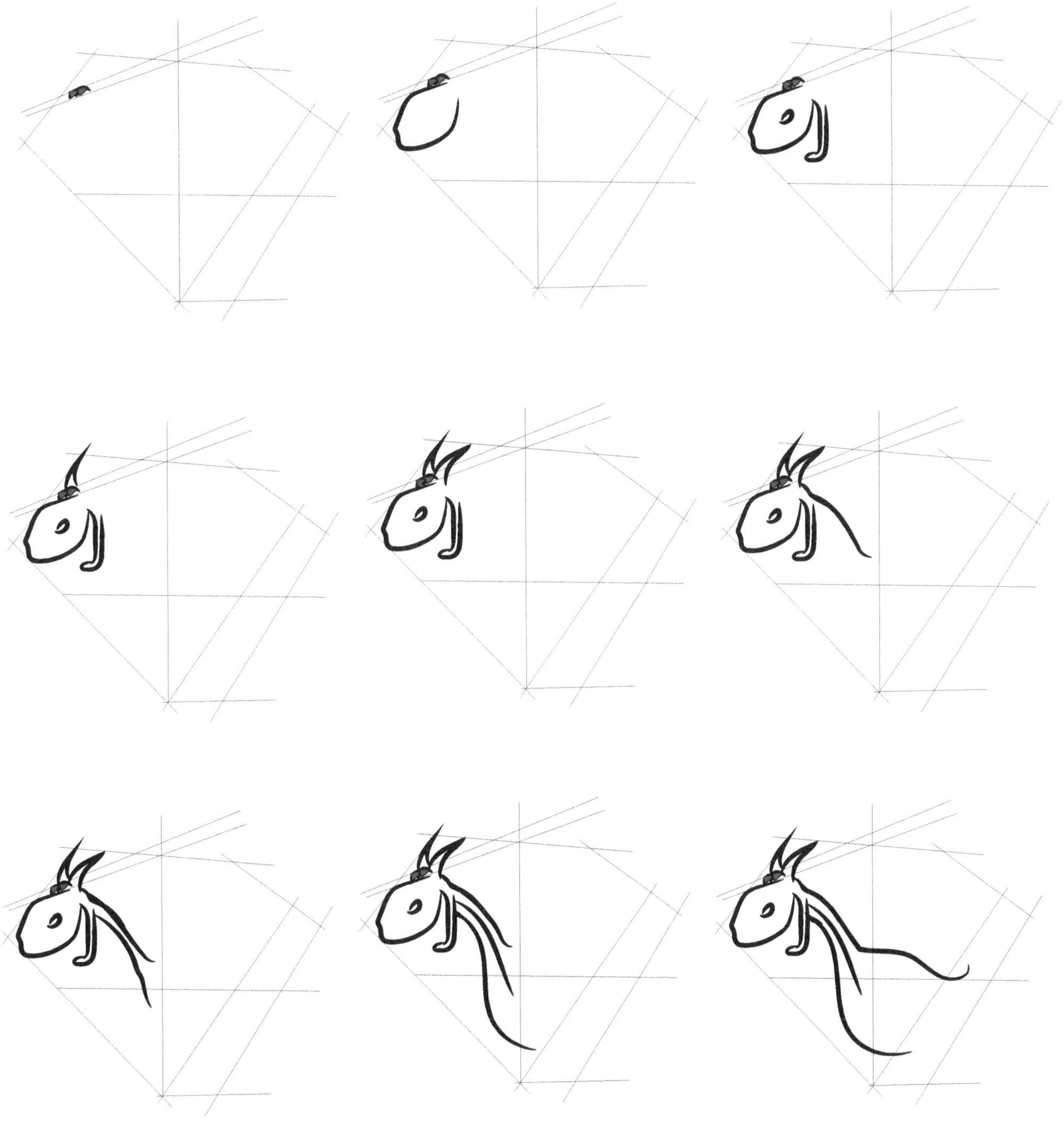

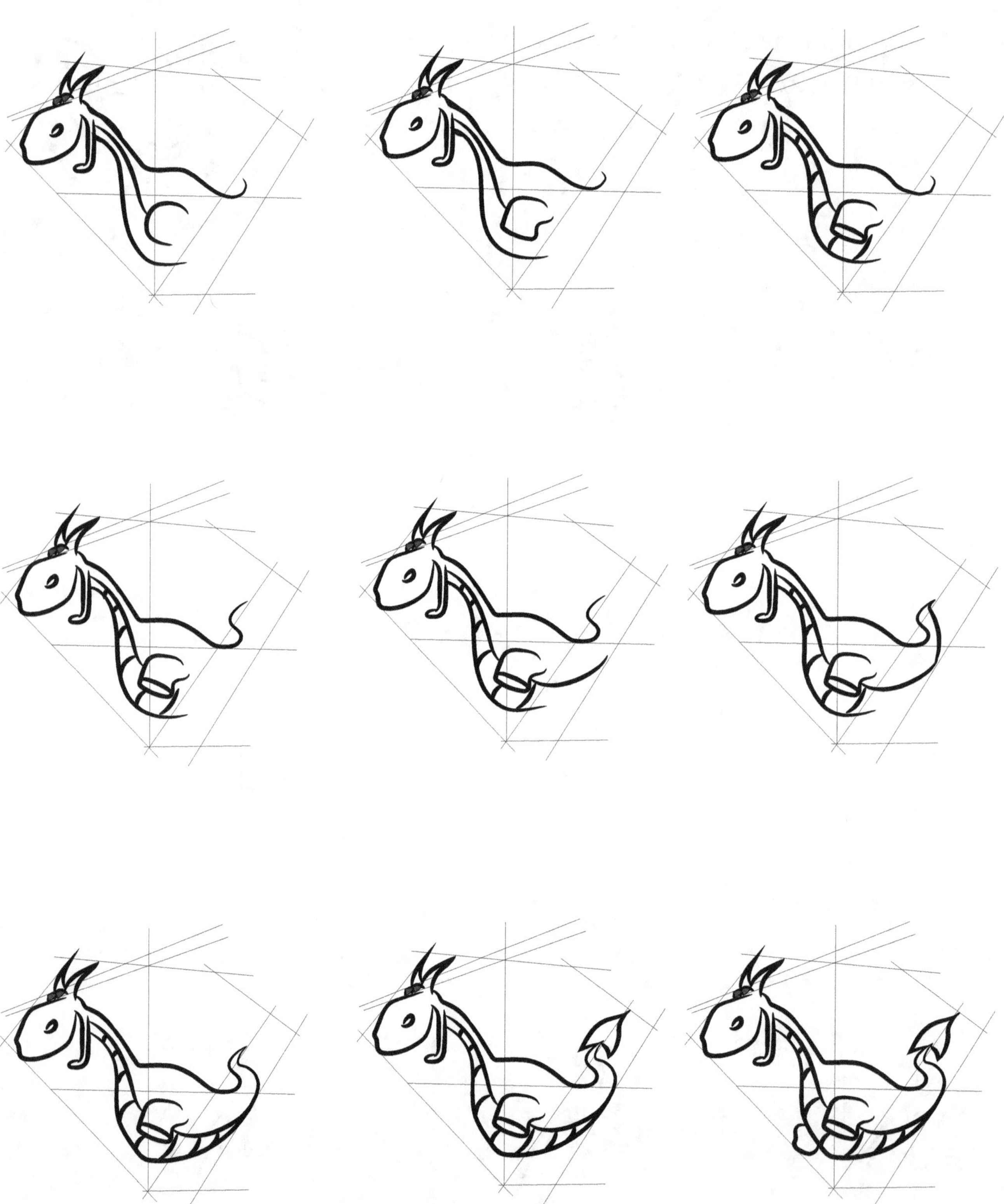

A B C D E F G H
1
2
3
4
5
6
7
8
9
10
11
12

18. The use of ellipses in your grid can bring curvature into your drawing.

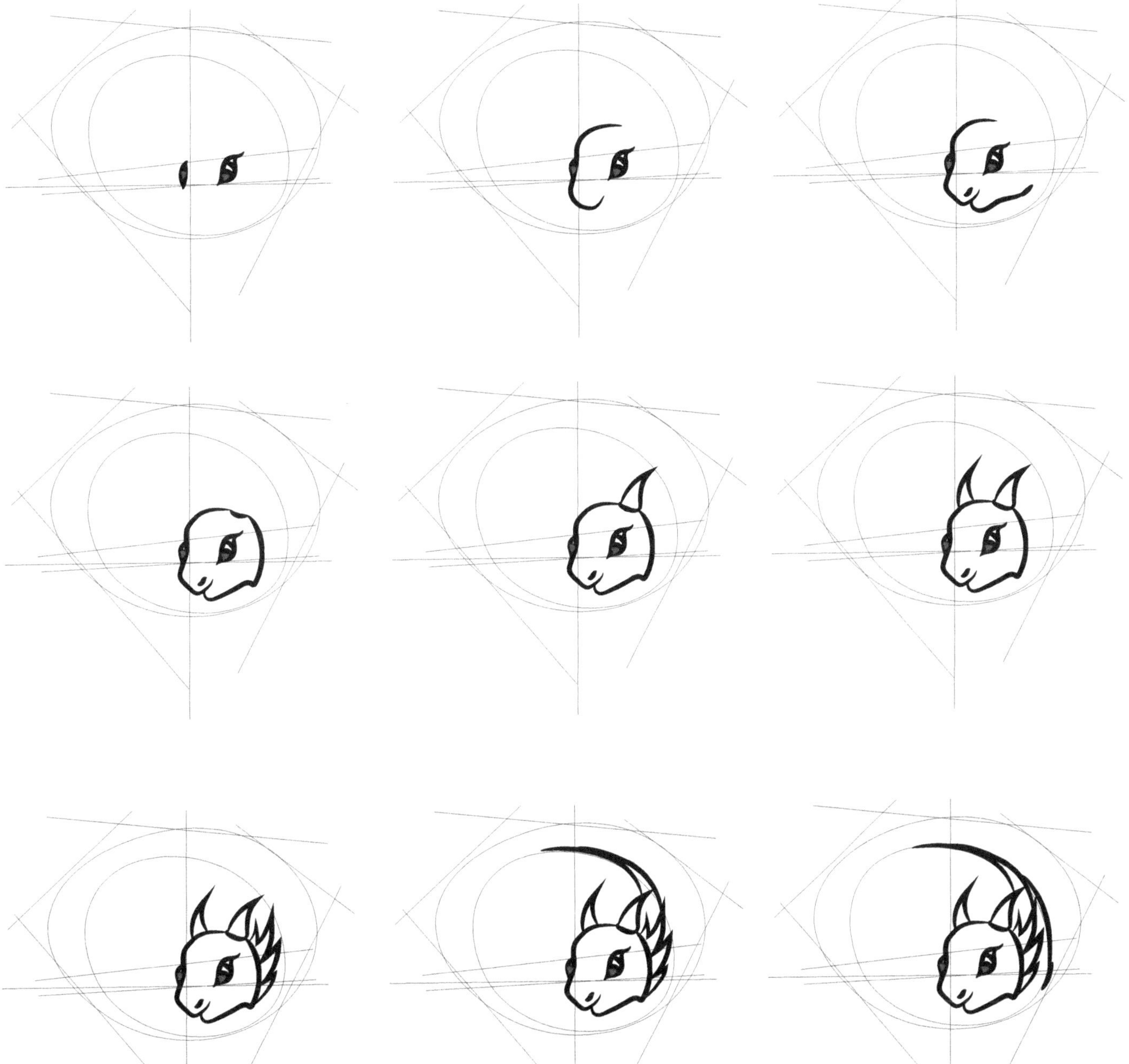

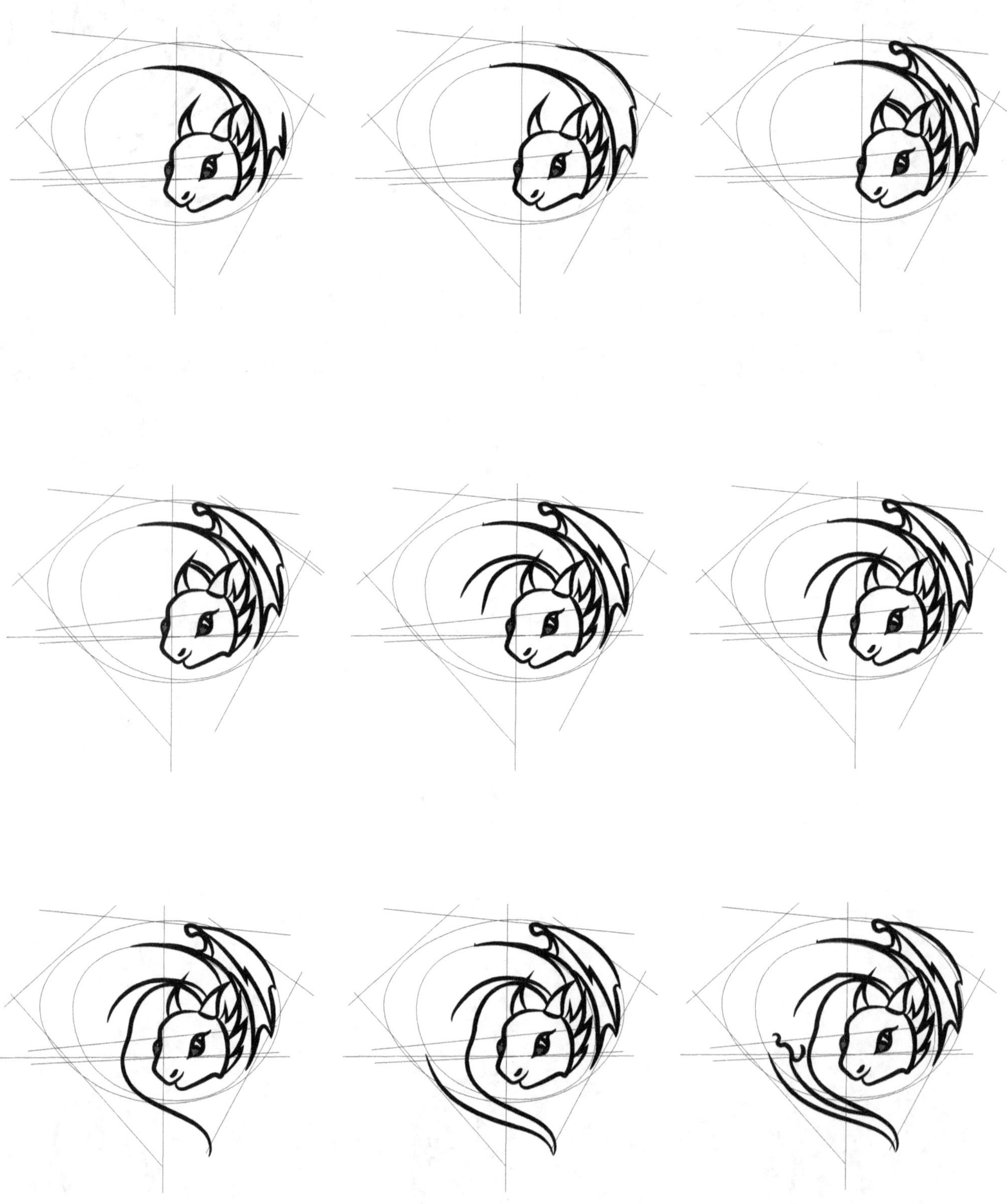

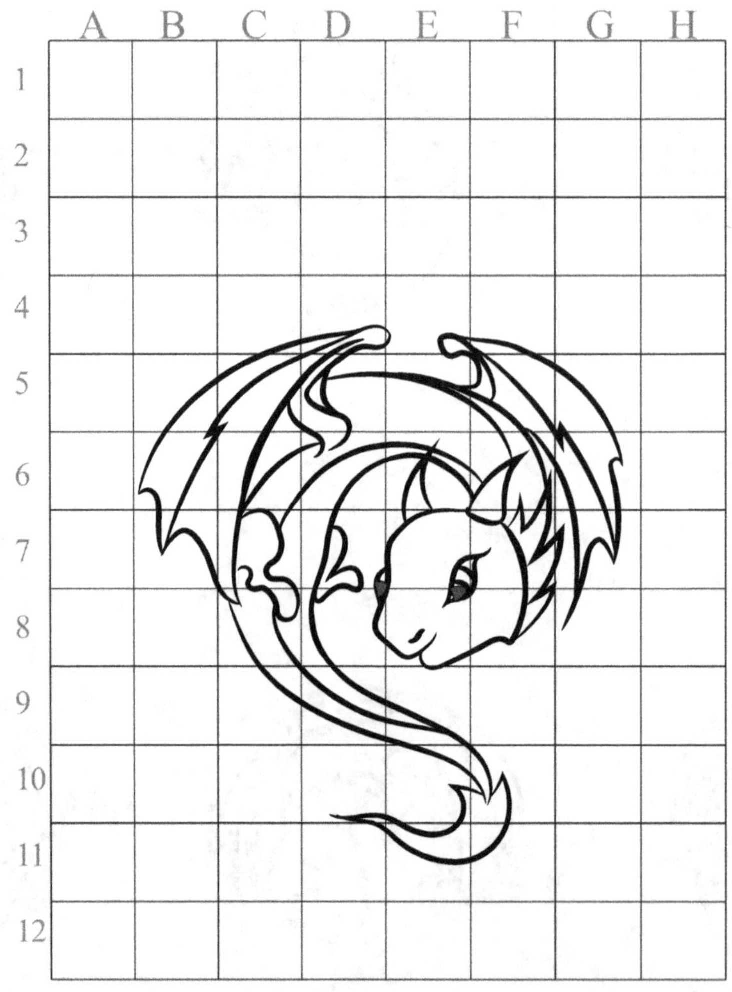

	A	B	C	D	E	F	G	H
1								
2								
3								
4								
5								
6								
7								
8								
9								
10								
11								
12								

19. The use of an ellipse in your initial grid can bring roundness to your drawing.

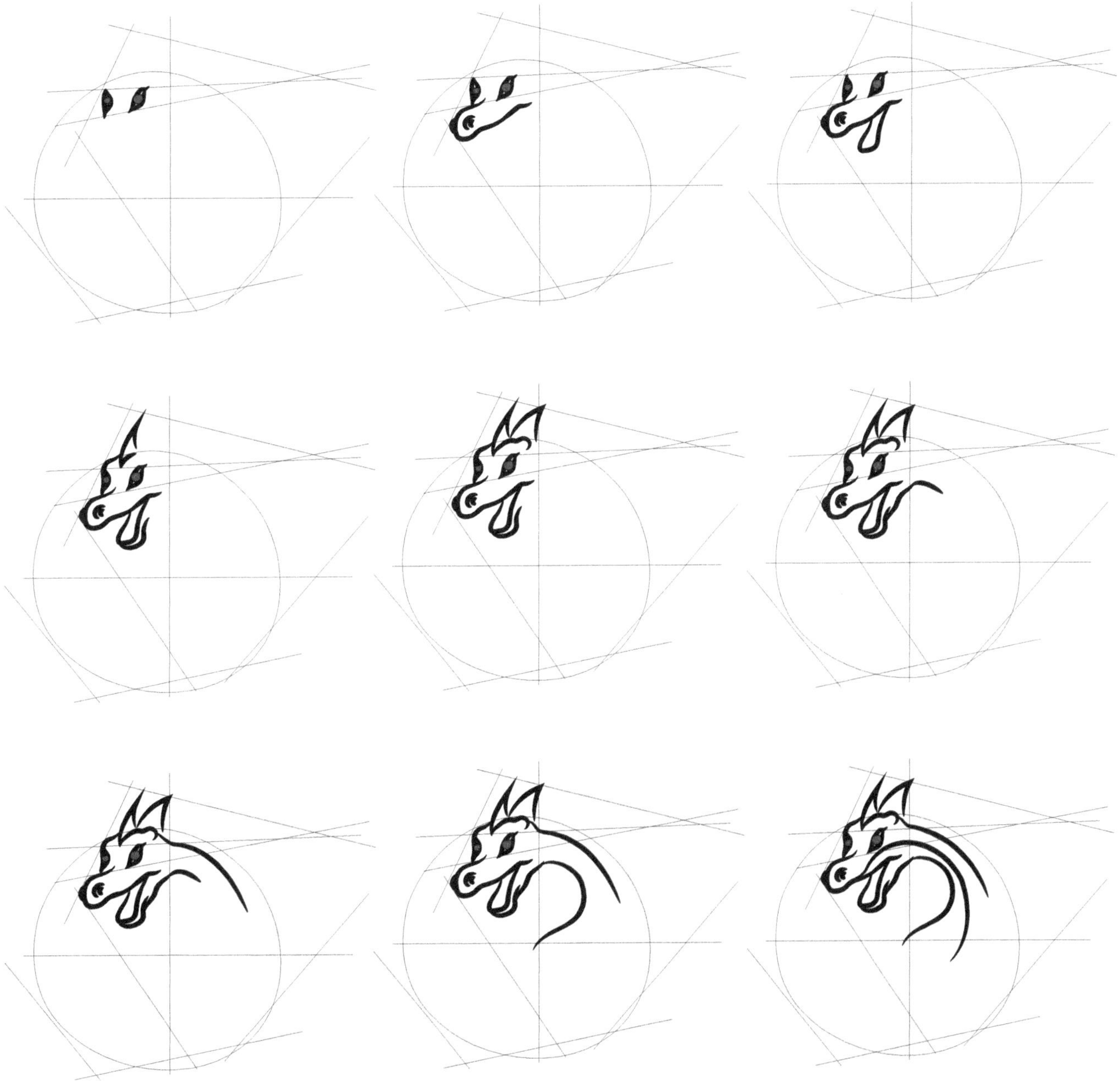

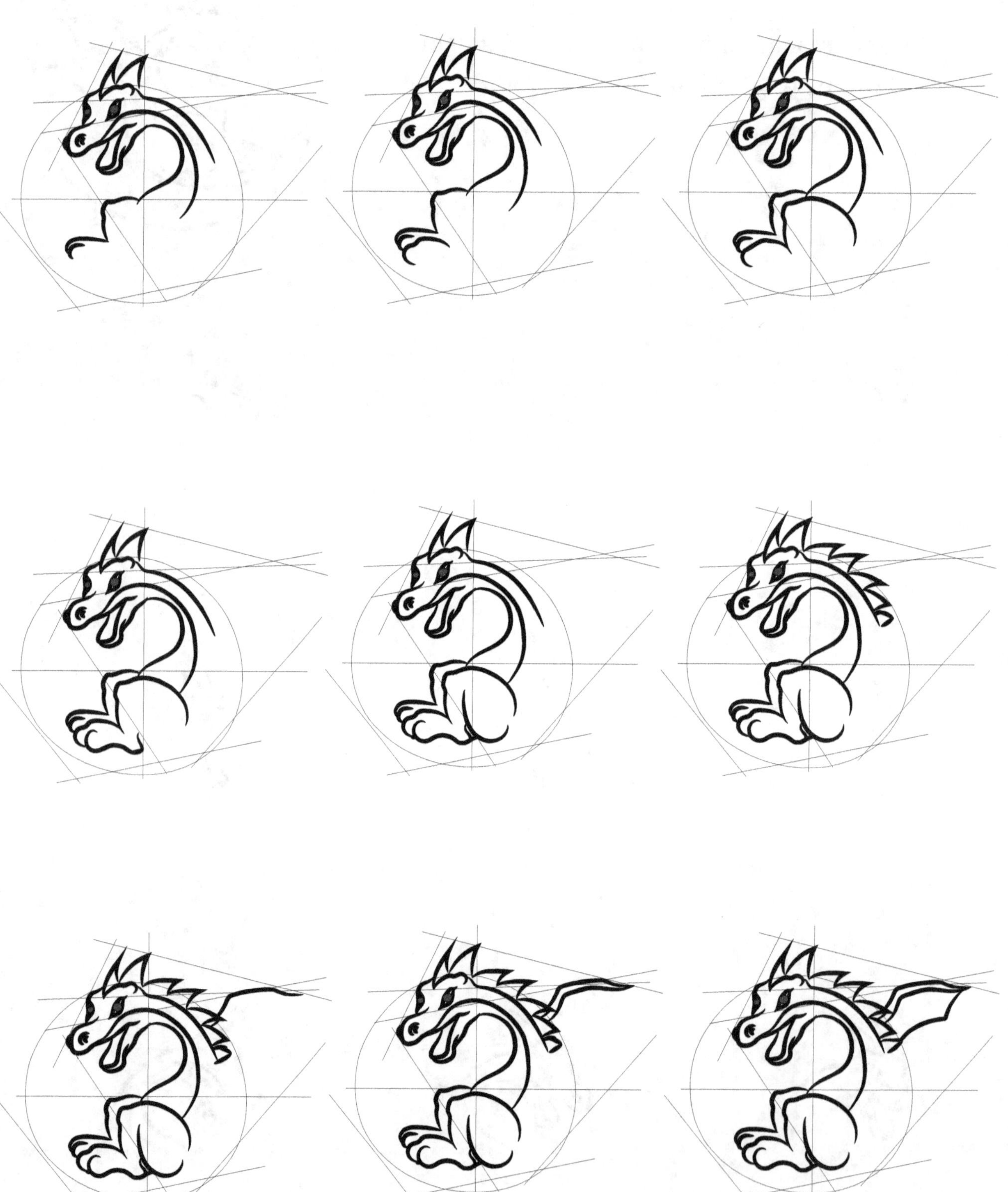

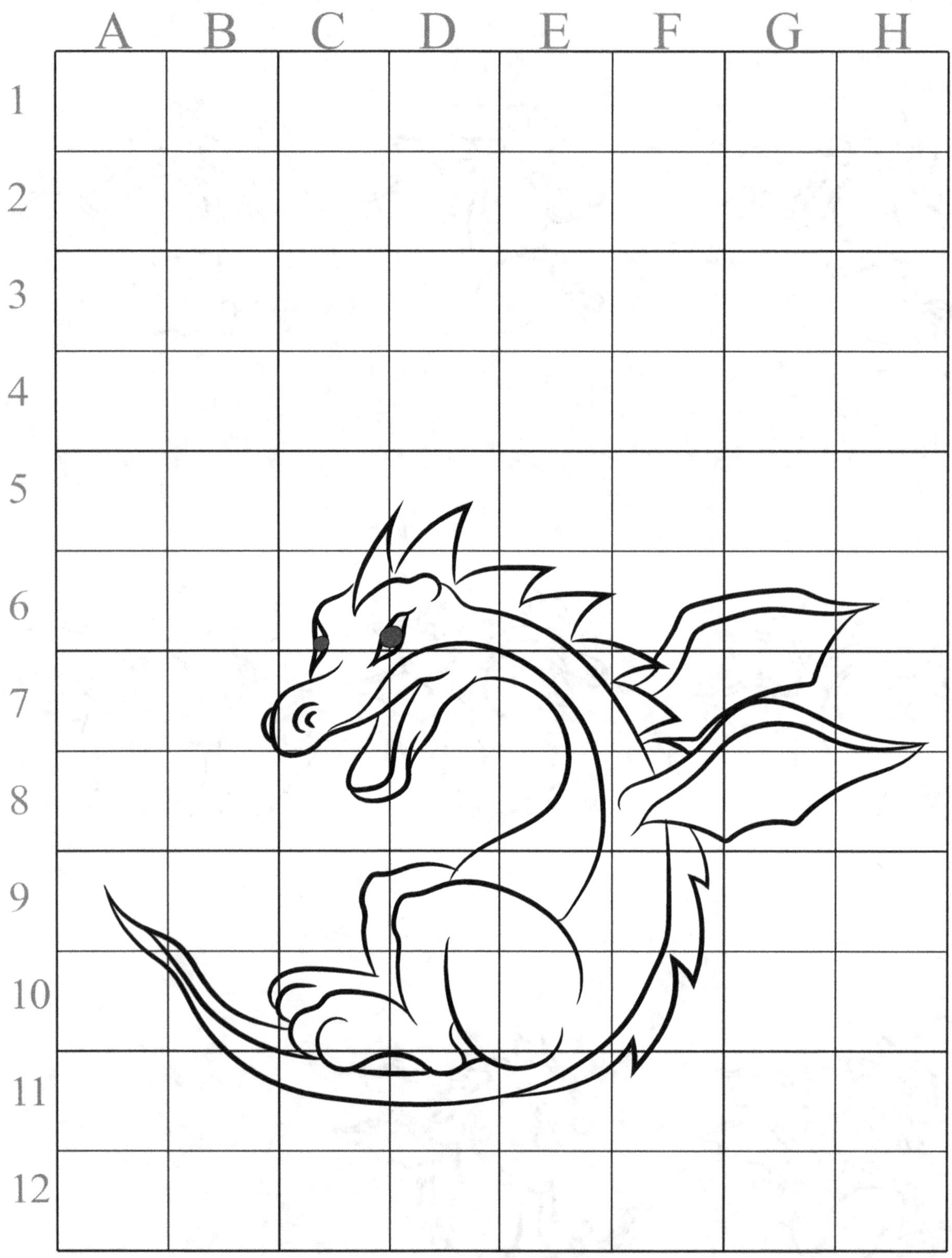

A B C D E F G H
1
2
3
4
5
6
7
8
9
10
11
12

20. There is no right way to draw a grid. It is a simple rough outline to get you started.

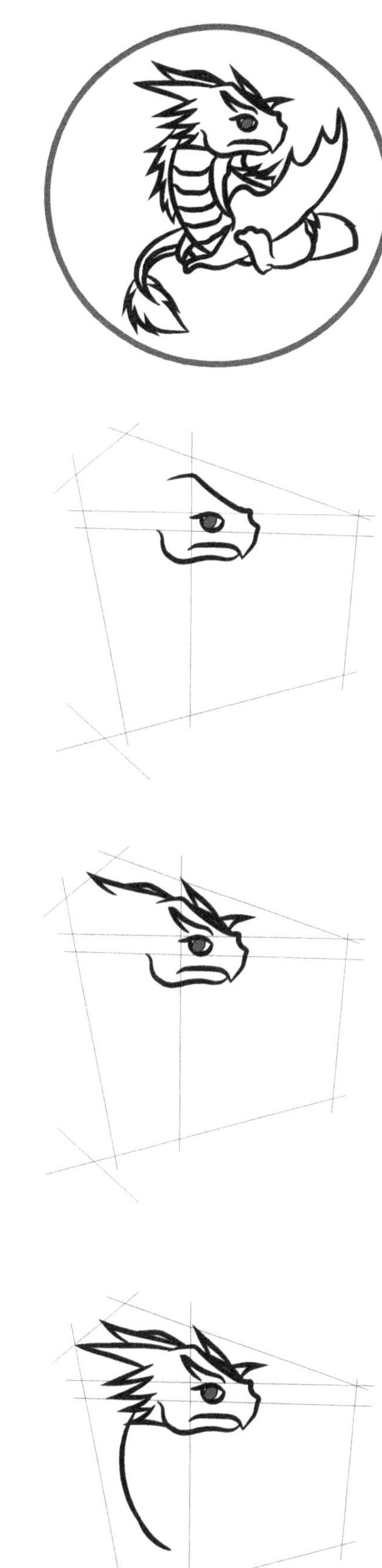

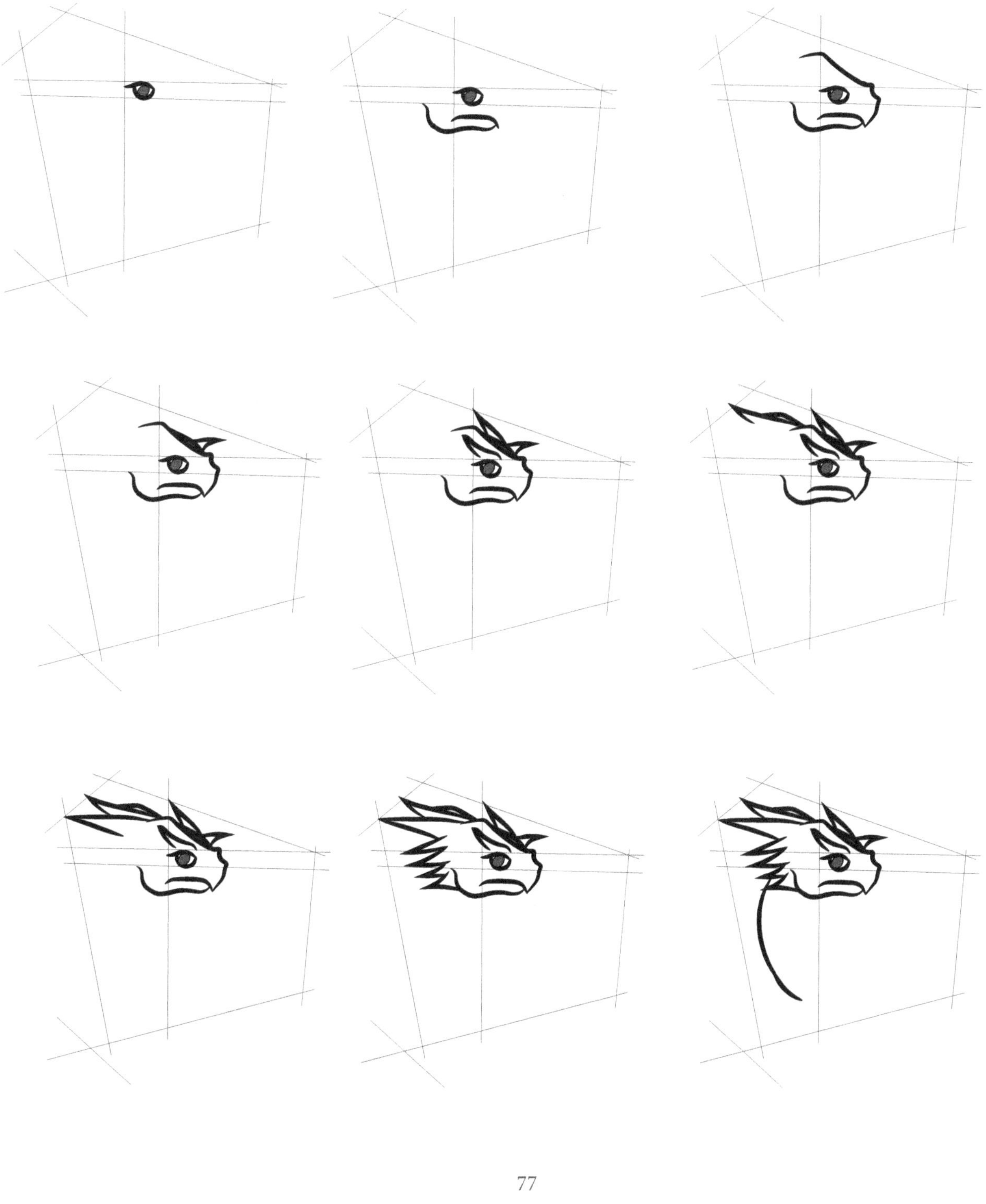

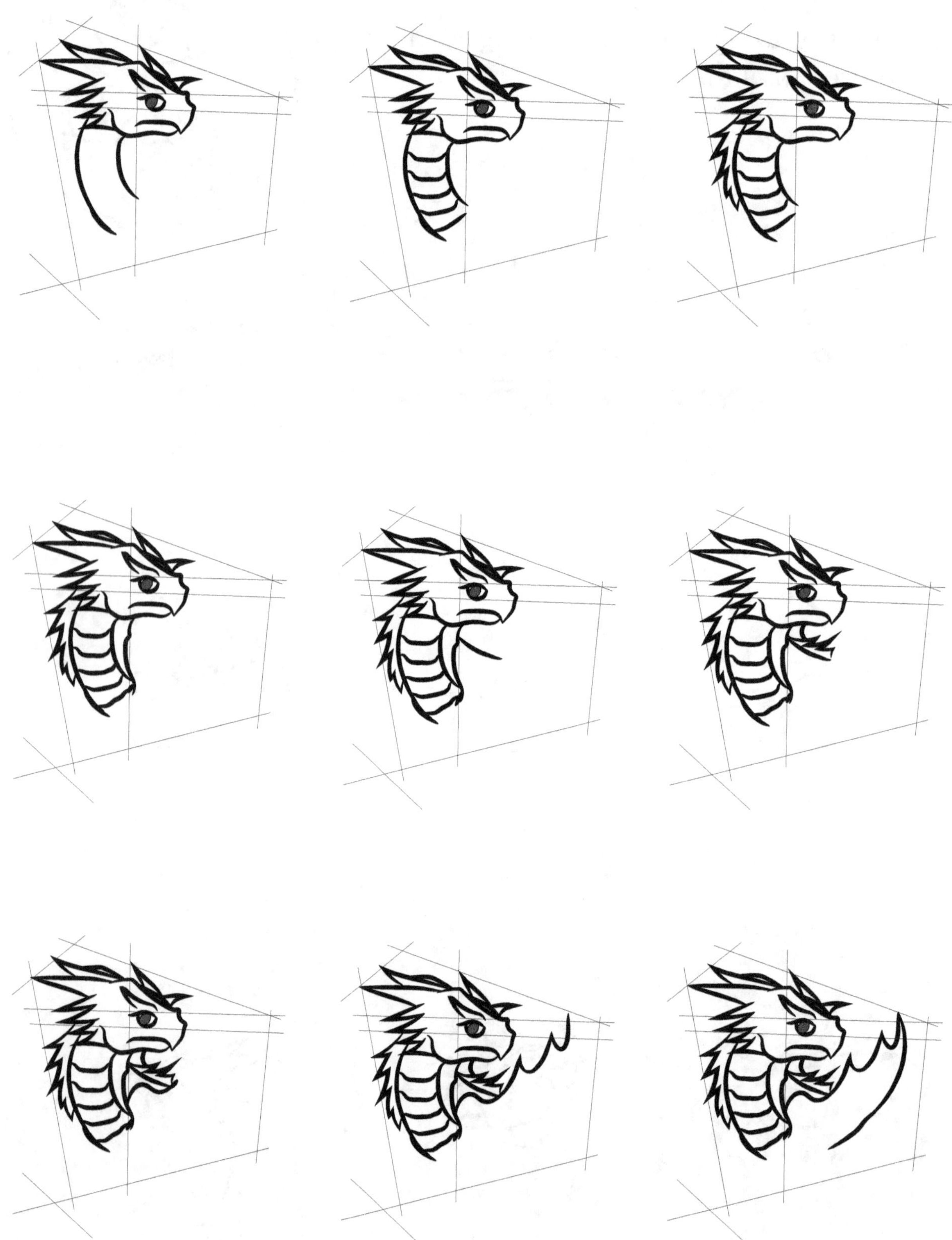

www.ingramcontent.com/pod-product-compliance
Lightning Source LLC
Chambersburg PA
CBHW081155130726
47996CB00009B/3138